Bottom up
BREAKTHROUGH

How to Drive Innovation from the Ground Up

———

A BOOK ON HOW BOTTOM-UP COMMUNICATION
CAN FOSTER A CULTURE OF INNOVATION

RICH DUNBAR

This book is a work of nonfiction. Any references to real people, organizations, or events are purely for informational or illustrative purposes. The views expressed in this book are those of the author and do not necessarily reflect any organization's official policy or position.

This book is dedicated to the memory of Devin Shillington, Ross Renee, Derrick Davidson and Mickael Deschênes

TABLE OF CONTENTS

FOREWORD

Nonprofit organizations like Support Services Group rely on strong leadership to drive change and achieve their missions. The SSG Board of Directors, likewise, is comprised of regional member representatives, family representatives, and community professionals, all passionate about improving the lives of members.

Allow me to introduce SSG Board of Directors Vice Chair Rich Dunbar, a Canadian military veteran, leader of innovation, and social impact strategist who heads up the Veterans Homelessness Project in Nova Scotia: collaborating with government, nonprofit, and private-sector organizations to help them innovate and grow. Rich is also a doctoral candidate in business administration, focusing on leadership and strategy.

His new book Bottom-Up Breakthrough offers a clear and practical approach to leadership that prioritizes people, detailing how engaging employees at every level can spark meaningful change and build stronger organizations.

Bottomup BREAKTHROUGH

In absorbing Rich's keen insight, I was reminded of the power that comes when leaders take time to truly listen, challenging me to reflect on how we approach innovation in our own organization.

SSG is proud of Rich's work and thrilled to witness its impact, with all book proceeds donated to Landing Strong, a Nova Scotia-based non-profit that provides mental health support to military veterans and first responders.

I wholeheartedly support this important work in promoting bottom-up innovation. Congratulations, Rich, and thank you for your ongoing dedication.

Mariana Manole-Baker (she/her) Executive Director

Support Services Group Cooperative Ltd

INTRODUCTION

The most dangerous phrase in any organization is:

"This is how we've always done it."

REAR ADMIRAL GRACE HOPPER

Hi, I'm Rich. With nearly two decades of service spanning both the Army and the Air Force, I've lived through the institutional rigidity and operational pressures that make—or break—innovation. I've seen how frontline insight often outpaces policy, and how transformative change usually starts with a simple question: Why are we doing it this way? The stories and strategies in this book aren't borrowed—they're built from the ground up, shaped by experience in high-stakes environments where innovation wasn't optional—it was essential.

Innovation isn't about resources—it's about mindset and action. This book explores how any organization—whether a business, government, startup, or nonprofit—can harness the power of bottom-up innovation. These strategies have been tested in high-stakes environments and proven in practice.

I first witnessed these principles in the military, where rigid structures often stifled change. Later, I applied them in an entirely different setting, assisting homeless veterans. That journey reinforced a powerful truth: Innovation isn't about rank, funding, or bureaucracy. It's about people.

The individuals closest to the problem hold the key to the solution—if only they are empowered to take action. "Innovation isn't about being the smartest person in the room—it's about being bold enough to ask, 'Why not?'"

This book isn't about theories. It's about real stories, struggles, and solutions—proving that when people think differently, they redefine the game.

The Cyclone's Unique Challenge: A Lesson in Supply and Demand

At 12 Wing, I quickly learned that logistical challenges could ground even the most sophisticated aircraft. The Cyclone's biggest issue was that its supply chain was broken. Unlike other RCAF aircraft, the Cyclone wasn't built for a single-customer supply chain. The manufacturer, Sikorsky, had planned to sell this helicopter to multiple nations. However, when Canada became its sole customer, the global supply chain it relied on never materialized.

This meant we operated on an On-Demand supply model—parts were only ordered when needed rather than stocked. On paper, this seemed efficient. In practice, it was a disaster. Imagine trying to fix a sophisticated aircraft—only to wait weeks, even months, for a critical part.

This presented a significant challenge; it highlighted the need to reevaluate how we provide support to keep the Cyclone in the air.

💡 **Lessons Learned**

- The people on the ground know best. As technicians and maintainers live and breathe these challenges daily, ignoring their insights means ignoring the best solutions.
- The Cyclone's technology was impressive, but technology alone wasn't enough. If we truly wanted to keep this aircraft in the air, we had to rethink how we supported it on the ground.

The Power of Bottom-Up Innovation in Government Organizations

Now, let's talk about something that plagues almost every organization:

- ➢ Top-down decision-making
- ➢ Slow decision-making
- ➢ Communication silos

Military organizations function like most prominent organizations, where all significant decisions stem from senior leadership at the top. The existing system functions successfully in numerous situations, although it needs consideration for specific matters.

But here's the issue: Does every decision have to originate from the top?

My previous role was as a member of the RCAF's Innovation Team, Plan Qulliq (PQ). PQ is based at NDHQ and has the enormous mandate of elevating innovation efforts within the entirety of the RCAF. The original team consisted of a Team Lead, Deputy Team Lead and four team members.

I recall sitting in a PQ meeting when Brigadier General Kiever, who was the Director General (DG) of the RCAF's Air & Space Division at the time. He was also the DG responsible for the creation of PQ.

He raised a pressing concern: communication silos. Information wasn't flowing properly. Instead of key projects within the RCAF operating collaboratively to reduce organizational waste, they operated in isolation. This could lead to duplicate efforts and wasted resources.

The General's observation revealed a fundamental weakness of the RCAF's top-down decision-making processes. Senior leaders at the strategic level sought answers from soldiers at the operational level, but the front-line workers could not relay their feedback to leaders.

Excellent ideas did not receive attention because they lacked a direct link to decision-makers, and the existing system failed to capture their insights and feedback.

🎇 The Good Idea Fairy: Where Innovation Goes to Die

In the military, we joke about the "Good Idea Fairy"—that magical place where great ideas go to die.

The reality?

If a junior member had a brilliant idea, it would rarely make it up to the chain of command, not because leadership didn't care but because the system wasn't designed to listen. That changed with rcafé.

☕ rcafé: The Innovation Game-Changer

rcafé was the first actual bottom-up innovation framework in the RCAF.

It was simple but revolutionary:

- ➤ Think Reddit but for the Air Force.
- ➤ Members could post questions, share solutions, and engage directly with senior leadership.
- ➤ Ideas didn't need to go through a dozen layers of the chain of command—they could be seen and acted on instantly.

For the first time, individuals at every level of the RCAF had an opportunity to contribute, innovate, and shape the future. This demonstrated something incredibly vital: bottom-up innovation isn't just essential in government organizations—it's necessary.

💡 Lessons Learned

- 🔨 A rigid hierarchy kills innovation. If only senior leaders make decisions, you miss out on the best ideas.
- 🔨 Breaking down communication silos saves time and money. If teams can't collaborate, they waste resources and slow down progress.
- 🔨 When people feel heard, they contribute more. If you give people ownership, they become active problem solvers instead of passive employees.

12 Wing: From Idea to Execution

What happens when you put an idea into action? At 12 Wing, we had limited resources but believed that providing people with the tools and space to solve their problems leads to success.

This book showcases real examples of bottom-up innovation, from saving thousands of hours through minor process changes to cultural innovations.

These are practical strategies that apply across military, corporate, and non-profit sectors. Innovation goes beyond technology and efficiency—it's about empowering people and transforming engagement at every level.

And that's precisely what this book is about.

THE CORE THEMES OF THIS BOOK

This book is structured around three main concepts:

Agency

Consider yourself in a position where you can make a significant impact. You are not simply an employee working under someone else's idea and bringing it to reality. You might lead a team of experts; your decisions are vital to business growth.

Having agency means that people have autonomy to determine what and how things are done, and they are motivated and proactive. Simply put, people are more productive, creative, and interested in making things work when they can control how things are done.

This is what we refer to as an agency.

Bottom-Up Communication

Bottom-up communication is a flow of communication from employees or lower levels of an organization to upper management or leadership. It allows frontline workers, teams, or individuals to share ideas, concerns, and feedback that influence decision-making and innovation.

In the age of command-and-control management, it is all too common to assume that vital information and ideas trickle down from the top. This is a very narrow mindset.

When all employees, regardless of the organization's hierarchy, can provide feedback and ideas, more thoughtful and incredible solutions can be achieved. This is called bottom-up communication.

Continuous Improvement

Continuous Improvement (CI) is an ongoing effort to enhance products, services, processes, or operations through small, incremental changes rather than large-scale transformations. It is a core principle in Lean, Agile, and Kaizen methodologies and focuses on efficiency, quality, and innovation.

Think of it like saving money; a few dollars here and there may seem insignificant, but they add up to a lot over time. Adopting this mindset allows us to remain proactive in problem-solving, whether the challenge is big or small.

These three concepts—agency, bottom-up communication, and continuous improvement, form the fundamentals of this book. These strategies helped us completely redesign our workplace, and they should also assist you in transforming yours.

How to Use This Book for Maximum Impact

This isn't just a book you read—it's a book you apply. As you turn each page, you'll discover:

◇ Real Stories from the Field

Learn from our experiences, including the lessons we've learned the hard way. These real-life examples illustrate challenges faced and overcame, turning the abstract into something practical.

◇ Practical Takeaways

Discover practical strategies you can implement immediately. Whether you aim to optimize a process or inspire innovation within your team, these insights are crafted for instant application.

◇ A Framework for Change

If you're leading a corporate team, managing a project office, or working in a mission-driven organization, you'll find strategies here that apply directly to your work. Bottom-up innovation is a force multiplier whether you're optimizing business processes, developing products, or improving social systems. This book will show you how to use it to unlock your team's full potential.

Let's dive in.

CHAPTER 1

THE BIRTH OF THE 12 WING INNOVATION PROGRAM

"The way to get started is to quit talking and begin doing."

WALT DISNEY

At 12 Wing, everyday work came with challenges that had long been accepted as "just the way things are." Our regular activities were crammed with minor yet stubborn challenges that formed an integral part of our systems, thus making progress seem almost impossible.

One of the biggest challenges? The CH-148 Cyclone.

As I watched a Cyclone hover during a test flight, I noticed the technicians nearby exchanging quiet conversations, some shaking their heads, others letting out frustrated sighs. Something was wrong.

Bottomup BREAKTHROUGH

At first, it seemed like a routine day, but the frustration on the technicians' faces told a different story. I approached them to ask what was going on, and that's when I learned about one of the biggest operational problems at 12 Wing: our supply chain appeared broken.

Unlike other RCAF aircraft, the Cyclone wasn't built for a single-customer supply chain. The manufacturer, Sikorsky, had anticipated selling this helicopter to multiple nations. When Canada became its sole customer, the global supply chain it relied on never materialized.

This left us with an On-Demand supply model—parts were ordered only when needed instead of stocked in warehouses. On paper, this seemed efficient. In practice, it was a disaster. Imagine trying to fix a sophisticated aircraft only to wait weeks—or even months—for a critical part. Our technicians faced this daily.

At that moment, it was clear that this wasn't just a minor inconvenience. It was a fundamental obstacle in our logistics system. We had to find a new approach to keep the Cyclone mission-ready.

I thought back to when I was a member of the RCAF innovation team, Plan Qulliq. I saw challenges like this as opportunities. In PQ, our role was to find innovative solutions that bridged the gaps in operations.

That's when I realized that innovation at 12 Wing wouldn't come from new technology alone. It would come from solving real-world problems with creative solutions from those who worked on or supported the aircraft.

This chapter is about moving from a resignation mindset to a proactive change—the 12 Wing Innovation Program with **no** financial resources.

Our journey was not about dramatic overhauls. We challenged traditional ways while trying to make incremental improvements. We realized that every small change, every minor tweak in our process, could add up to something much more significant over time. These little yet impactful improvements generated a successive transformation that modified our entire organization's culture.

This approach isn't unique to military settings. Businesses that foster innovation don't rely on top-down mandates; they encourage team-driven improvements. Companies like **Toyota** revolutionized manufacturing by allowing frontline workers to suggest small, incremental changes that transformed global supply chains.

Start-ups like **Airbnb** and **Uber** didn't wait for perfect conditions; they built simple solutions, tested them quickly, and iterated based on actual user feedback. Whether in a corporate boardroom, a tech start-up, or a social impact organization, bottom-up innovation is a powerful driver of change.

In this chapter, I'll share how a dedicated team decided to change the 12 Wings approach. We refocused our energy from logistical issues we could not control and shifted it towards improvements that would enhance our day-to-day operations.

What follows is the story of that transformation: a journey from systemic challenges to actionable solutions. It is a story of tenacity, teamwork, and faith in innovation that proves no change is too small to make a meaningful impact.

As I later discovered, these lessons weren't just valuable in a military setting—they applied anywhere teams were solving problems. When I later transitioned from military innovation to working with veterans experiencing homelessness, I used the same principles:

- Questioning existing systems,
- Testing small interventions before scaling; and
- Empowering those closest to the issue to drive solutions.

Innovation isn't about rank, structure, or industry, it's about mindset. The same framework that transformed operations at 12 Wing could just as easily be used to streamline workflows in a corporate Project Management Office (PMO), improve customer experience in a start-up, or create better support systems in social services. As we'll see in this book, that's exactly what's happening.

Join me as we explore how our commitment to improving everyday practices eventually led to creating an innovation program that redefined how work gets done at 12 Wing—one practical step at a time.

Shifting Focus: From Systemic Challenges to Actionable Solutions

Military, corporate, or non-profit organizations often struggle with deeply embedded inefficiencies that feel normal. At 12 Wing, we regularly faced operational delays that were out of our control.

The same pattern exists in corporate environments, where slow decision-making bottlenecks innovation or start-ups, where scaling challenges overwhelm early momentum. No matter the setting, breaking through these systemic barriers requires the same approach: questioning assumptions, testing practical solutions, and empowering teams to take ownership of change.

Our efforts started with adopting a different point of view. Instead of seeing these problems as unchangeable parts of the system, we began to ask ourselves:

> *"What if we could break them down into smaller pieces?"*

We studied large issues to recognize that each contained multiple minor problems we could handle. Seeing these problems divided into smaller parts unlocked the chance to handle each element one at a time.

Our analysis revealed that several complex procedures needed simplification because their basic activities were completed over extended periods. Specific examination of separate steps allowed us to generate solutions for their optimization process. We achieved our breakthrough when we understood that enhancing any minor segment could make the whole process more efficient.

When we first started, we asked numerous questions during each discussion.

- How could we make our work more efficient?
- What steps were causing the most delay?
- Where were the bottlenecks that made it nearly impossible to move forward?

By asking these questions, our organization could pinpoint specific areas for improvement. Fostering this type of thinking allowed our colleagues to leverage strategic questioning, which would later open the door to a flood of innovative ideas for both small and large improvements at our workplace.

The beauty of this approach was that it allowed everyone in the workplace to contribute. It wasn't just the senior officers or the managers making decisions. All personnel at all levels were invited to offer their thoughts and suggestions. The technicians conveyed detailed information regarding problems during their work tasks. When they spoke up, their suggestions were not only heard—they were valued. The bottom-up problem-solving approach eliminated hierarchical obstacles, creating an environment for unimpeded idea-sharing among the whole team.

Some solutions involved reorganizing how parts were ordered, while others focused on improving communication between departments. Every minor fix contributed to reducing the overall delay. This proved that even a massive problem can be tackled effectively when focused on actionable solutions.

At the same time, our organization has shifted its perspective on innovative solutions. We found that the concept of continuous improvement motivates staff members to consistently seek better approaches, even if the results may be minimal. These diverse approaches led the organization to avoid passive behaviour and adopt proactive, systems-based problem-solving methods. The daily work environment offered our members opportunities to enhance operational excellence.

As we made these small changes, the overall culture shifted. People felt empowered because they saw that their ideas could lead to real improvements. The systemic challenges didn't diminish their ability to take control of things and design solutions that benefited everyone. This new energy was contagious.

It became evident to everyone in our organization that transformation was achievable and employees had the tools necessary to impact their workplace positively. This shift in attitude was significant, as it demonstrated that the initiative was not merely a program—it was fully integrated into our work processes.

In this chapter, I want you to see that the journey from systemic challenges to actionable solutions is not a dramatic, overnight transformation. It is a gradual process of peeling back the layers of a complex problem and addressing each piece, one at a time. It's about recognizing that every small step counts and that these steps can significantly change how an organization works.

💡 Lessons Learned

- 📌 Overcoming systemic problems is tricky. Dissect them in manageable chunks via a step-by-step approach to solve even the most challenging issues.
- 📌 Swift, massive transformation isn't practical and rife with risks. Small, incremental changes (e.g., process tweaks, improved communication, or digital tool implementation) can create long-lasting impacts.
- 📌 Seek employee ideas from all corners of an organization rather than relying solely on leadership.

Innovation in Action

12 Wing's Innovation Team experienced firsthand that real change happens from within organizations, not just at the top. Their approach to solving logistical challenges demonstrated that innovation isn't dependent on large budgets or major infrastructure changes, it thrives when individuals take the initiative and commit to continuous improvement.

The success of 12 Wing's Innovation Team proves that determined individuals can drive transformation, even with limited resources. They created lasting change by leveraging existing systems, embracing creative problem-solving, and fostering a culture of innovation.

This book shares actual stories of these principles in action, offering insights that may inspire transformation in your work environment. Small improvements, made consistently, lead to remarkable progress.

The Spark: Pitching an Innovation Team via Email

A regular email catalyzed massive changes at 12 Wing by generating an idea that ultimately reshaped it. I opened my inbox one typical morning and scrolled until I noticed a message that would alter the course of 12 Wing. The Wing's emails usually contain updates, reminders, or news about ongoing changes in the area.

One email sent indirectly from Maj Veenhof distinguished itself from all the others that day. One phrase from the message captured my attention.

"We would like your feedback!"

Overthinking felt trivial, so I started composing my response quickly. Interestingly, my first suggestion was related to the survey format itself. I proposed that the Wing hold small focus groups to discuss key issues. After sending my response, I thought my email might get lost among the many others that had likely piled up in the recipient's inbox.

But then, something remarkable happened. One of the 12 Wings' senior leaders, Maj Veenhof, replied almost immediately. His brief response went directly to organizing a meeting.

A few weeks after his reply, I met with him. As the meeting began, I noticed that he paid close attention to my suggestions, wrote down notes, and nodded, showing that he was actively listening as I spoke. He displayed a genuine interest in everything I shared.

Then came the turning point. I asked, "What if we created an innovation cell? A dedicated group to tackle inefficiencies, explore new technologies, and improve 12 Wing?"

I still remember that moment vividly.

As I spoke, I could see his pen come to a sudden halt, and his eyes widened in a way that said he was thinking, "**This is something different.**"

It wasn't just another suggestion but a proposal that could change how we operated. After the meeting, our lives took an unexpected turn. Maj Veenhof departed for deployment while I started nine months of parental leave for my second daughter, Jillian. The concept remained untouched for months.

When we finally reconnected, something surprising happened. The vision for an innovation team was still alive. If anything, it had grown stronger. As time passed, Maj Veenhof became known to me as Nick.

Nick and I held countless meetings to refine our plan for pitching the creation of an innovation team to the Wing Commander, the strategic head of our organization. We explored potential challenges and drafted solutions. With each discussion and meeting, our vision became clearer.

I noticed several important things while looking back at that experience.

Opportunities often hide in plain sight

Sometimes, a simple line in an email can be the spark that ignites something much more significant. That one sentence from an otherwise typical email wasn't just a casual remark, it was a challenge to all of us to start thinking differently. It reminded me that great opportunities don't always come with fanfare; sometimes, they come quietly, nestled among the everyday details of our work.

Act fast

That chance might have slipped away if I had hesitated or second-guessed myself. Ideas can be lost in the shuffle in our busy environment if we don't act on them quickly. Maj Veenhof's prompt response showed me that when you seize the moment and act, the impact can be immediate and decisive.

Collaboration is everything

No idea survives in isolation. My initial email was just the beginning. Our idea of an innovation team evolved into a solid proposal through working together— listening, refining, and building on each other's thoughts. Nick's collaboration was crucial. With his help, we transformed a raw concept into a clear, actionable plan.

This experience taught me that innovation isn't about waiting for a miracle to happen. It's about recognizing a small opportunity, acting on it immediately, and then working with others to develop that idea into something tangible. It's a reminder that any organization always has room for new ideas—no matter how structured or bureaucratic. The key is to listen, act, and collaborate.

So, when you think about your work, consider this:

"Every day, you have a chance to make a difference."

A single email, a brief conversation, or a small suggestion can be the start of something transformative. The story of pitching an innovation team at 12 Wing isn't just about a proposal but the power of taking the initiative. It's about looking beyond the routine and seeing potential where others see only the status quo.

Remember, change starts with you. Stay open to possibilities, whether in a meeting, at your desk, or even casually checking your email. When an opportunity presents itself, please don't SKIP it. Act on it, discuss it with your peers, and be ready to refine your ideas. Your insights, no matter how small they may seem, could be the spark that leads to significant improvements in your work environment.

Ultimately, an idea alone mattered, the journey from a simple suggestion to a shared vision of change. It was the willingness to take a risk, propose something different, and rally others around that idea. That spark in my inbox lit the flame for an innovation program that changed how we worked, and it all began with a single invitation to share ideas.

As you progress in your projects or within your organization, take this story as a reminder: sometimes, a minor action can create a chain reaction that leads to real, lasting change.

Your ideas matter whether you're on your front lines or working behind the scenes. They have the potential to turn everyday challenges into opportunities for improvement. All it takes is the courage to speak up and the readiness to collaborate with others who share your vision.

And that's the heart of what we're trying to achieve. A culture of innovation where every member feels empowered to contribute. It's a culture built on the belief that no idea is too small and that every voice counts. The spark that started with that one email is a testament to what can happen when we all decide to take a chance on something new.

Let this be a call to action for you as well. Keep your eyes open for those moments when a small idea can lead to significant change. Be ready to act when opportunities arise, and always remember that collaboration is key. Together, we can build an environment where innovation isn't a buzzword, it's a way of life.

💡 Lessons Learned

- 📌 A single unexpected invitation, like a simple email line, can unlock opportunities hidden in daily tasks. Grab such chances without hesitation, knowing the smallest prompt can spur decisive change.
- 📌 Unpursued ideas lose their magic, so act swiftly and decisively. Waiting or second-guessing means missing out on chances to transform challenges into tangible improvements.
- 📌 No idea flourishes in isolation. Innovation thrives when individuals unite, share insights, and refine concepts collectively, with diverse perspectives and support igniting the sparks of progress.

Endorsement & Buy-In

Another turning point came when Nick arranged a meeting with the Wing Commander, Colonel Holmes, and the Wing Chief, Chief Warrant Officer Wezenbeek. This was our opportunity to secure senior leadership buy-in for our innovation team.

As I stepped into the meeting, I faced Col Holmes, or "Homer," as his peers knew him, while CWO Wezenbeek sat across from him. Their authority was undeniable, both were widely respected for their experience, wisdom, and leadership and I felt privileged to be in that room.

Bottomup BREAKTHROUGH

Nick had entrusted me with leading the presentation, a responsibility that carried weight. I took a deep breath, recalling my time with PQ. At PQ, I worked under LCol Baldasaro (Diane) and Capt Pohran (Andrew), and together, they showed me the power of strategic thinking, teamwork, and trust. Diane had built her team on both rank and potential, and Andrew had introduced structured agile processes that transformed our meetings into efficient problem-solving sessions.

Those experiences gave me the confidence I needed. I had done this work before and knew how to present a vision, gain buy-in, and inspire action. I finished my breath, and I began.

I explained the need for an innovation team within the Wing and how it needed to be focused on developing practical solutions to everyday inefficiencies. The program would harness bottom-up communication, ensuring that 12 Wing personnel had a platform to contribute ideas and drive positive change.

As I spoke, I noticed Col Holmes and CWO Wezenbeek's engagement. Their attentive posture and the Chief's detailed note-taking reassured me that our proposal resonated. Then, after a brief pause, a subtle nod between them signalled what I had hoped for—we had secured their endorsement.

The foundation for 12 Wing's Innovation Charter was set with their support. This wasn't just an idea anymore—it was a mandate for action.

Bottomup BREAKTHROUGH

💡 Lessons Learned

- 🔨 **Champion Potential:** Great teams are built on the skills and vision of their members, leaders like Col. Holmes and CWO Wezenbeek seeing potential beyond hierarchy and titles. Promising ideas can originate anywhere, so seek talent and creativity in unexpected places.

- 🔨 **Seek a Mentor(s):** LCol Baldasaro and Capt Pohran (my mentors) helped me grow, their advice emphasizing bottom-up communication and unexpected opportunities. Choose mentors who will likewise support you as the key to meaningful change.

- 🔨 **Build Confidence:** Confidence develops via experience; my belief in 12 Wing's Innovation Team is reinforced by the experience I gained at PQ. Use your training to grow in your tasks and your belief in your own ideas, inspiring others.

- 🔨 **Communicate Clearly:** Per Col Holmes and CWO Wezenbeek, effectively communicating your vision helps motivate others without divulging details—their support an organic response to a thoughtful proposal. Present your ideas clearly and simply, with clarity as your strongest ally.

- 🔨 **Seize the Moment:** Opportunities are rare, and decisive action is powerful. Don't let fear hold you back; if you see an opening, take it (despite an unknown outcome), as doing so can mean the difference between a missed chance and a potential breakthrough.

When I exited the room, I realized through this experience that the concept meant more than an abstract idea. The 12 Wing Charter Nick and I would eventually draft would create an official commitment to reshape how 12 Wings' innovation culture. The backing received from our senior leaders indicated we would make significant advancements in our journey ahead.

Drafting the Innovation Charter

A charter is a formal document that defines a team's mission, goals, roles, and responsibilities, providing clear direction and accountability. For an innovation team, a charter is crucial because it establishes authority, alignment, and a shared vision, ensuring that creative ideas translate into actionable solutions with measurable impact.

Drafting the first Innovation Charter for 12 Wing became my responsibility, although it was a collaborative effort. The charter creation required Nick and I to leverage existing resources instead of developing something new while maximizing their performance.

I remember when I first volunteered for the job. My thinking then remained straightforward: How do I leverage existing tools and experiences? My time at Plan Qulliq gave me a deep knowledge of innovation, which I intended to expand into new opportunities.

I remember when I was at PQ; we conducted an RCAF-wide survey to measure the pulse of innovation within the RCAF. Through a data-driven approach, PQ wanted to understand the opinions of all Air Force personnel on innovation. We wanted to know what was working, what wasn't, and whether people even knew about initiatives like the RCAF Commander's Vector Check, the RCAF's version of a "**Dragon's Den**" where RCAF members could pitch an idea directly to the RCAF Commander!

PQ also wanted to analyze successful and failing policies and procedures and measure awareness of RCAF-based programs and initiatives. The survey data provided essential insights into the problems and challenges facing RCAF members performing their duties at the operational level.

With my experience at PQ at the top of my mind, I started working on the Charter and discovered that most of the necessary information for its creation was already present. I had:

- **Survey Responses:** These weren't just numbers on a page; they were genuine insights from 12 Wing members, telling me exactly where the frustrations lay and what they needed most.
- **Plan Qulliq's Terms of Reference:** This document details how innovation teams were previously set up. It provides a clear structure that I can adapt to our needs at 12 Wing.
- **The RCAF Innovation Charter:** This charter served as a high-level framework, giving me the overarching principles and goals to align with. It was like having a blueprint that showed the bigger picture.

- **PQ's Communications Plan:** I knew that for the Charter to work, it couldn't just sit on a shelf collecting dust. It needed to be a living document—a tool to drive real change by keeping everyone informed and engaged.
- **Academic Research:** A little bit of theory never hurt anyone. I sprinkled in insights from my academic studies, reinforcing why bottom-up innovation was so important, especially in structured organizations like the military.

Utilizing all these resources, I put pen to paper and began crafting the first draft. I produced an initial rather large version of the Charter, which specified everyone's exact duties, writing the first draft marked only the start of my work. Nick and I dedicated our time for weeks to revising every document section. Our mission was to ensure that the entire document presented itself as transparent, actionable content before moving forward with the approval process by our senior leaders, Col Holmes and CWO Wezenbeek.

As Nick and I molded the charter to our organization's needs, we realized it was about creating a foundation—a blueprint for how innovation would be structured and sustained at 12 Wing for years to come.

Nick had taught me that every detail, every line we wrote, had to serve a purpose. We weren't just trying to make a good impression; we were building a tool to empower our Wing and potentially the RCAF towards real, lasting change.

💡 Lessons Learned

- 🔨 **Use Existing Resources:** Why start from scratch? Nick and I scaled down existing documents from a strategic to an operational level for our charter draft. Combining existing information with previous lessons fuels new ideas and effective solutions.

- 🔨 **Make Data-Driven Decisions to Boost Legitimacy:** PQ survey data helped us create a charter based on 12 Wing member feedback; this customization feeds document authenticity and effectiveness in addressing current issues.

- 🔨 **Collaboration to Boost Quality:** Nick and I leveraged insights from Col Holmes and CWO Wezenbeek for document optimization, transforming our draft into a solid innovation plan; collaboration produces better results than individual effort.

A thoughtfully structured organizational charter drives individuals beyond mere process documentation, igniting their motivation for implementation. The final approved draft revealed that we had created something that surpassed simple document status. This innovation guide we developed acted as a strategic decision-making tool to steer the change initiatives at 12 Wing and clarify the responsibilities of its members in fostering beneficial transformations.

My experience during this process has led me to offer some insights about it.

◇ Don't Overthink It

You need to write down your ideas when you already have sufficient resources to work from. Start working without delaying your initiative because all elements are not without flaws. A first draft provides the foundation that eventually transforms through continuous development during the creative work process.

◇ Focus on Clarity and Action

The entire plan and Charter require actionable statements in each part. What essential actions does this message require of anyone who reads it? The question for readers becomes what action steps they should take following this information. Rephrase your content until you create statements that clearly express your audience's instructions.

◇ Listen to Your Team

Your team members and colleagues will provide you with valuable feedback. Their experiences make their advice exceptional. Your plan will require teamwork to reach its full potential, even if you think you already have all the necessary answers. We can't always lead; take a step back and learn to follow to empower your team.

◇ Ground Your Ideas in Reality

Your vision needs the support of applicable data, survey results, and operational frameworks. Concrete evidence and established methods that demonstrate the validity of your concepts can make your organization's needs more convincing to others.

◇ **Think Long Term**

The plan should develop a system beyond solving present-day challenges to establish ongoing progress capabilities. Your plan must be flexible and adaptable to evolve through new emerging challenges.

Bringing Best Practices to 12 Wing

When I transitioned from NDHQ to 12 Wing, I quickly recognized a familiar challenge, the need to break down communication silos; my time at PQ had already proven that connecting strategic leadership with operational personnel was critical for solving real problems. PQ demonstrated how a structured, agile approach could bridge this gap, and I saw an opportunity to apply those lessons at 12 Wing.

At PQ, I learned that identifying problems wasn't enough—we needed a new method to transform insights into action. One key takeaway was agile project management, which changed how I viewed policy implementation. Instead of waiting for a "perfect" solution through traditional phased planning (a waterfall approach), we adopted an agile mindset— starting small, iterating, and refining based on real-time feedback.

A major tool we used was Minimum Viable Products (MVPs), small-scale, functional solutions designed for rapid testing and improvement. Rather than lengthy approval processes, we concentrated on launching an initial version, gathering feedback, and adjusting based on user experience.

This was precisely what 12 Wing required. Leadership had already validated our innovation concept, and our task was to turn it into an executable strategy.

Fostering Innovation at 12 Wing

At 12 Wing, Nick and I established a fully operational innovation team without requesting additional funding or personnel. Instead, we built a volunteer-based initiative where people who wanted to drive change could step forward.

This method followed three key principles:

1. **Lean Structure –** The 12 Wing innovation team was built without additional funding or staff positions. A shared dedication to change allowed us to cut through red tape and accelerate decision-making.
2. **Iterative Process –** We started small. Town halls with 12 Wing personnel provided insights on inefficiencies, which we tested and refined in real-time. Each stage informed the next, leading to incremental but lasting improvements.
3. **Bottom-Up Innovation –** The best ideas don't always come from senior leaders. Operational personnel working directly with the systems had the most practical insights. By giving them a voice, we ensured that solutions were designed by those who understood the problems firsthand.

Bottomup BREAKTHROUGH

The success of this approach reinforced key insights about what truly drives innovation—not rigid top-down directives but adaptable strategies, engaged individuals, and continuous learning. These lessons shaped how we approached problem-solving at 12 Wing and provided a framework that can be applied to any organization.

💡 **Lessons Learned**

- 🔨 **Top-Down Solutions Rarely Succeed Alone:** All organizational levels must adapt senior leaders' strategic plans, NDHQ's robust plan gaining effectiveness via practical steps involving everyone.

- 🔨 **MVPs Extend Beyond Tech:** Grounded in Eric Ries's The Lean Startup, Minimum Viable Product (MVP) applications extend beyond tech for internal policy/procedural refinements. Small-scale product tests and feedback procurement save resources and reduce risk up front.

- 🔨 **Passion Drives Innovation:** Dedicated volunteers often outperform well-funded teams that may lack motivation. Truly committing to innovation leads to continuous improvement among engaged individuals.

- 🔨 **Agile Principles Drive Success:** Agile project management highlights flexible, quick cycle methods as the key to success. After gathering insights with a basic version of your idea, you optimize to reduce project time and reap better results per real user feedback.

Bottomup BREAKTHROUGH

🔑 Key Takeaways

- 🔒 **Bottom-Up Ideas:** Innovation starts at all levels. Front-line workers provide valuable insights to improve operations. Empowering them leads to better solutions and boosts morale.
- 🔒 **Break Down Problems:** Don't feel overwhelmed by large issues. Split them into smaller, manageable parts and find simple solutions.
- 🔒 **Start Small:** Use a Minimum Viable Product (MVP) to test ideas. Gather feedback and gradually expand, protecting your investments.
- 🔒 **Encourage Communication:** Create an environment where employees can share thoughts openly. Remove barriers to their voices and value their contributions.
- 🔒 **Build a Passionate Team:** Surround yourself with motivated individuals who are eager to make a positive impact, as they deliver better results than a disengaged larger team.
- 🔒 **Stay Flexible:** Innovation is a continuous process. Be ready to adapt your methods based on new feedback and changes in the business environment.

These lessons made one clear: innovation doesn't occur accidentally—it occurs when organizations actively cultivate a culture that encourages it. Having great ideas isn't sufficient.

Next, we'll explore building a culture where innovation isn't just allowed—but actively encouraged.

CHAPTER 2

FOSTERING A BOTTOM-UP INNOVATION CULTURE

"The people who are crazy enough to think they can change the world are the ones who do."

STEVE JOBS

According to a study by **Sideways 6**, over 50% of employees feel that their companies fail to implement good ideas. This perception is often attributed to traditional top-down decision-making processes, where organizational hierarchies limit the flow of ideas from employees to management. Such structures can discourage employees from sharing their insights, making valuable suggestions overlooked.

In many organizations, ideas seem to flow only from the top down—decisions are made in high-level offices, and everyone else is expected to follow orders. But at 12 Wing, we discovered that the real power to drive change lies with those out in the field daily. In this chapter, we'll explore how we built a culture where innovation starts at the grassroots, where every voice is valued, and where small ideas can spark significant changes.

Fostering a bottom-up innovation culture requires more action than waiting for executive commands. Every team member, from aircraft technicians to office personnel supporting operational flows, plays a vital role in unlocking their creative potential with us. Frontline employees often possess insights that senior executives, distanced from daily operations, may overlook. The thoughtful ideas presented by employees become essential components leading to lasting improvements.

Our approach was straightforward yet effective. We established open dialogue channels through different communication platforms while building internal feedback platforms at all organizational levels. We shifted towards creating an environment that allowed ideas to emerge from every area of our organization. When individuals realize that their thoughts matter while being heard by the organization, they become significantly more motivated to work on future solutions.

This chapter explains our methods for building this up-and-downward organizational culture. Our strategies involve arranging casual town hall meetings and using digital suggestion boxes alongside scheduled team meetings to enable personnel suggestions. Team meetings serve as more than formal gatherings since they allow members to transform their frustrations into new creative solutions.

Real success stories will emerge from the base through testimonies about how technicians submit ideas that transform processes or when casual conversation-generated breakthroughs streamline operations. Compiling numerous small innovations defines true business transformation since innovation works through aggregating diverse minor advancements.

The discussion includes our practical difficulties as well. A traditionally structured organization faces significant challenges in establishing bottom-up innovation across its culture. The transformation met occasional obstacles because the existing practices sometimes appeared fixed in their ways. Each barrier became an instruction for personal growth and organizational adjustment. Building a bottom-up organizational culture requires sustained, focused listening and earned trust, and it takes extended periods for any business to succeed in current fast-changing conditions.

The following information should demonstrate that innovation exists for everyone regardless of title or organizational level. It's a collective effort. Everyone who wants to enable their team or share frontline ideas understands that their ideas matter fundamentally for success. The following section presents principles of a bottom-up culture and specific guidelines for their practical application to your current workplace.

I will explain our process of changing corporate thinking, fostering open dialogue, and developing a team environment that gives all members significant influence over change. The essence of our innovation path demonstrates that authentic transformation occurs through workplace ingenuity starting from inside the system. Ideas develop one by one.

What is Bottom-Up Innovation?

Let's talk about bottom-up innovation. It allows organizations to discover creative solutions through decisions that originate below executive positions without dependency on top-level managers. The system promotes frontline personnel and all organizational members to present their understanding and innovative solutions for advancement.

The best innovative ideas emerge from all organizational personnel, regardless of their professional standing or position. People who encounter daily challenges have an essential role to play in the managerial decision-making process. Every day, workers who interact with organizational challenges possess distinct understandings of potential improvement areas because of their direct problem observation.

The concept plays out this way, according to my explanation:

Imagine a Busy Workshop

A machine shop with active employees is a practical example of this method. Daily technicians detect several minor issues that could enhance the machine's operational efficiency, even though the manager holds a general plan for the machine. Bottom-up innovation lets the technicians directly express their ideas for improvements in the system. Everyone within the system can engage their valuable input since their contributions hold worth.

Not Just a Top-Down Directive

Most business organizations receive their directives from senior management positions. The organizational leaders establish policies that all workers must follow. That's a top-down approach. Bottom-up innovation flips that idea. Inside every organization, ideas should originate from the bottom level until they reach the top. People who feel their feedback has value will likely present novel solutions.

❓ Why It Matters

The advantage of bottom-up innovation still raises questions. People who directly experience the problem possess the best capability to find practical solutions for their day-to-day challenges. A person who faces a consistent challenge will likely discover practical solutions for their difficulty. Organizations that use the vast array of existing employee knowledge can undertake proven solutions that will endure over time.

At 12 Wing, we discovered that maintenance technicians interacting with the equipment and aircraft daily provided numerous recommendations for modifying procedures for streamlining operations. Team members' proposed solutions came from practical insights obtained while handling actual operational challenges. These employees' engagement resulted in time-efficient solutions, decreased error frequency, and enhanced employee remuneration.

Characteristics of Bottom-Up Innovation

◇ Inclusivity

All team members acquire equal opportunities to present their thoughts, whether their position is a manager or technician. Each worker, from the manager to the technician level, provides essential knowledge through their unique professional views. The inclusive approach produces a wide array of innovative ideas that come from different perspectives.

◇ Collaboration

The bottom-up innovation process unlocks potential from all levels of an organization. It pairs junior and senior members together to develop ideas, with an experienced mentor leading to unique and creative solutions.

◇ Empowerment

Employee empowerment rises when people realize their thoughts generate concrete organizational modifications. The empowerment system produces benefits that transform the workplace environment and bring continuous improvement into organizational norms.

◇ Practical Solutions for Real Challenges

Staff members' concepts are grounded in genuine operational problems. These work models address real issues at the operational level. Focused and practical solutions are more likely to succeed during implementation.

How It Works in Practice

I will illustrate a typical workplace situation.

Managing parts in aircraft maintenance demands careful attention. Technicians who frequently handle parts grasp the procedures associated with part management. A junior technician proposes reorganizing storage locations to enhance efficiency.

The above idea would be refined with a senior peer or facilitator until it is ready to be pitched to an approving authority at a strategic level, someone who can authorize or fund the idea. The solution will be implemented as a minimum viable product (MVP) if approved. The priority is creating a product, process, or procedure that can be expanded and improved through experience, allowing continuous improvement.

Bottomup BREAKTHROUGH

Benefits of Bottom-Up Innovation

Speed: Since the people who identify the problem propose the solution, improvements can be made quickly.

Efficiency: The solutions are tailored to address real issues, which means they often work better in practice.

Engagement: Employees who feel that their ideas are valued become more engaged and invested in their work.

Adaptability: A bottom-up approach creates a culture where change is welcomed. This flexibility can be a significant asset in today's fast-changing world.

🗣 Practical Advice

- ☑ **Create Open Channels:** Use digital suggestion boxes, team meetings, online forums, or Share-Point to promote safe idea-sharing without fear of judgment.
- ☑ **Encourage Experimentation:** Allow controlled testing of simple, easy-to-implement ideas. An MVP strategy helps staff discover new initiatives through iterative changes.
- ☑ **Celebrate Successes:** Recognize and reward contributions to motivate innovation by showing how ideas lead to positive changes.
- ☑ **Lead by Example:** As a leader, be open to proposals from entry-level employees to inspire others to share their thoughts.

☑ **Provide Resources:** Support bottom-up innovation with minimal resources and encourage information exchange across all organizational levels.

Collecting ideas from staff is half the process, but it also requires a feedback mechanism. Future evaluations should assess implemented ideas to determine their effects before making improvements. The active feedback cycle advances processes while enabling organizations to respond quickly.

The organizational process of bottom-up innovation enables everyone within the organization to share their wisdom and best practices. This approach removes barriers that usually prevent valuable ideas from reaching senior leaders, allowing entry-level employees to communicate their first-hand insights. With this mindset, your organization becomes more productive as every member feels empowered to contribute, while collaborative solutions emerge from spontaneous conversations.

Your approach to innovation through bottom-up strategies allows you to develop organizational improvement and problem-solving solutions simultaneously. The basic yet essential philosophy states that organizational advancement involves everyone in improvement processes. Through this lesson, you will transform your workplace creation and improve your approach to solving problems in all your life domains.

Innovation isn't just for CEOs or managers; it begins with you. Take a look around your workplace. What small change could lead to a significant impact? Act today. Even minor suggestions can result in major improvements for any organization. Encouraging dialogue among all team members opens up limitless potential for positive transformation.

The Role of Agency

In an organizational context, agency refers to an individual's or team's capacity to make independent decisions, take initiative, and influence outcomes within their roles. It reflects autonomy, empowerment, and accountability in decision-making processes.

The pivotal notion that transformed our journey is the power of agency to make transformative changes.

In 2025, fast-paced organizations face a significant challenge in maintaining continuous motivation and employee engagement over extended periods. The ongoing need to replace members due to medical releases, retirements, and other factors presents a fundamental issue, as organizations must retain experienced talent while attracting new candidates without losing current staff.

The solution that has always remained clear to me is **agency**. Leveraging agency within an organization empowers the workforce to create a professional atmosphere and work environment. Individuals who feel that their input matters will shift from merely performing their jobs to actively solving problems and contributing positively to organizational growth.

There are essential reasons why agency remains vital to all workplaces.

The Link Between Agency and Retention

People involved in decision-making get more value from the company. I've seen this myself. Granting 12 Wing members the power to suggest new ideas has made them happier at work. Their role in shaping future operations has turned them into active contributors.

Changing beliefs in this way helps keep employees. Employees who feel recognized for their contributions are likelier to stay with the company longer. While a salary is important, employees also want to celebrate their achievements and feel proud of their work daily. When their ideas are put into action, they become more committed to the organization's success. This sense of ownership turns regular jobs into fulfilling careers.

Recruitment Through Reputation

Employee actions greatly impact an organization's hiring process. When employees enjoy their work environment, they talk about it with others. For instance, team members leave meetings excited because their ideas lead to real changes. They happily share their positive experiences at 12 Wing with friends and potential job applicants. This kind of positive sharing can lead to significant improvements. The organization gains a better reputation, attracting new talent.

Such a positive work atmosphere drives overall success because every team member feels empowered. A good reputation helps organizations maintain their high standards as satisfied and motivated employees naturally draw in others who want to be part of their success story.

Empowerment Sparks Innovation

When employees are encouraged to propose and develop their ideas into effective solutions for themselves and their colleagues, it creates a sense of empowerment within the organization. A culture that empowers individuals can lead to significant positive changes through many small but impactful ideas.

💡 Lessons Learned

- 📌 **People Stay Where They Feel Valued:** Employees who feel in control and that their opinions matter are engaged contributors rather than mere cogs in a system, exhibiting more effort and loyalty knowing the influence of their ideas and thus boosting retention.
- 📌 **Culture Spreads via Word of Mouth:** A positive workplace attracts candidates organically; enthusiastic employees disseminate their energy to create a strong organizational pull.

🏷️ **Retention and Recruitment Are Linked:** Team satisfaction attracts new hires, and organizational appeal depends on staff happiness from feeling empowered at work, supporting current operations and long-term growth.

🗣️ Practical Advice

☑️ **Listen Actively:** Encourage open communication channels. Organizations should offer various ways for team members to share their ideas, ensuring everyone feels heard and valued.

☑️ **Encourage Ownership:** Assign clear tasks and give people the autonomy to make decisions related to their work. Allow them to lead their projects and make choices.

☑️ **Provide Growth Opportunities:** Support both immediate improvements and long-term development. Offer training, mentoring, and advancement options to motivate employees to reach their full potential.

☑️ **Foster Collaboration:** Break down silos and promote teamwork across departments. Collaboration enhances creativity and leads to better results than working alone.

☑️ **Lead by Example:** Leaders should model the behaviour they want to see, embracing new ideas and taking thoughtful risks. This builds respect and encourages everyone to engage.

☑ **The Bigger Picture:** To empower change and create an environment where everyone can contribute to success.

Organizations are most successful when they empower their workforce within today's dynamic business environment. The organization shows adaptability alongside innovation, leading to increased resilience. 12 Wing has proven that leadership, which encourages everyone to voice their opinions, brings ongoing benefits for all members.

Empowering employees to drive change enhances operations and creates significant organizational effects. True innovation arises from enabling people to lead changes that transform every aspect of the organization.

Overcoming Resistance: Addressing Skeptics

Many of my peers expressed their doubts during the establishment process of the 12 Wing Innovation Team, which required Nick and me to deal with such resistance. My mind holds an exact memory of voices proclaiming:

- "This won't amount to anything,"
- "This is not the way it works around here,"
- "Nothing will ever change."

I was told many initiatives disappeared into the ether, while people who witnessed these events made negative remarks about our initiative.

The decision not to embrace doubt was crucial because it proved not to be an obstacle to our goals. Whenever a new concept or process enters an established system, it creates a challenge caused by unfamiliarity. However, skepticism faded as we quickly implemented real progress, which swayed the once-disbelieving colleagues to begin participating in the Innovation program.

The process to achieve our breakthrough involves the following steps.

Show, Don't Just Tell

Words alone proved insufficient to change the minds of doubters within the organization. Results must be demonstrated to people instead of relying on promises and theories to garner their support. Our team focused on achieving several brief yet significant accomplishments every staff member could see.

Start Small, Deliver Early Wins

Regardless of their scale, we implemented visible improvements instead of promising a complete existing policy or procedure. Each quick win built trust, and we showcased these successes during our town halls. Since they experienced these benefits firsthand, the results were enough to sway even the most reluctant critics to reassess their assumptions.

Bottomup BREAKTHROUGH

Involve the Skeptics

Skeptics received an invitation rather than exclusion from the process—the individuals who promptly criticized solutions usually provided meaningful judgment on organization practices. The inclusion process enabled critics to become active participants, transforming them into supporters. Their contributions led to enhanced approach refinement, making them participants in the change rather than active opponents of change.

Recognize Contributions

Recognition is one of the significant factors that led people to support our initiatives. Early skeptics observed that successful ideas were credited to their colleagues, leading them to participate in the initiatives. The Innovation Portal transitioned from receiving ideas from select enthusiasts to receiving multiple inputs from all organization members.

🔑 Key Takeaways

- 🔒 When others doubt your plans, this should not be taken as a failure but as a way of testing your ideas through challenges.
- 🔒 People naturally resist changes when it happens.
- 🔒 The successful delivery of actual outcomes can shift skeptics to become believers more effectively than any amount of explanation presented alone.

Bottomup BREAKTHROUGH

🔒 The effort to achieve concrete outcomes should replace time-consuming arguments. People lose their doubts rapidly when they experience tangible enhancements that enhance their work activities.

🔒 One small success act can trigger extensive support and backing from others.

Give People a Reason to Buy In

Creating momentum fosters better resistance elimination than any other method. Staff members naturally want to participate in positive organizational transformations because they see their peers being recognized for implementing new concepts. Every success, regardless of magnitude, should be celebrated throughout your organization. Eventually, everyone will engage to avoid being outpaced by others.

🗣 Practical Advice

☑ Deliver Early Wins. Launch with initiatives that produce immediate advantages. Welcomed collaboration demonstrates that your ideas function as promised in practice and create trust between teams.

☑ Engage Everyone Establish various platforms that allow every team member to contribute their ideas. The process requires active engagement with all team members, including the critics, and hearing from enthusiastic voices. Their comments contain aspects that will help you improve your method.

Bottomup BREAKTHROUGH

☑ Be Persistent The path to change requires time because resistance is a natural part of this process. The first signs of resistance should not discourage you from continuing your attempts. The resistance should act as fuel to demonstrate that your innovations lead to actual valuable enhancements.

☑ Communicate Clearly You should maintain active communication channels. The transformation process requires initial explanations of the modifications, universal advantages, and continuous feedback opportunities. When organizations promote clear communication, they create faith among workers and lower their doubts.

💡 Lessons Learned

🔨 The transformation of doubtful conditions enables seamless change implementation.

🔨 People will eventually embrace your results, which they can sense and observe firsthand. Building such a culture strengthens team motivation for innovation and improvement efforts.

🔨 Accept that resistance will naturally appear on your path. The opposition demonstrates that your proposals have achieved enough credibility to warrant consideration.

The 1% Improvement Mindset: Small Changes, Big Impact

The **1% Improvement Mindset** stems from the Kaizen philosophy, a Japanese concept of "continuous improvement." However, it gained widespread recognition through British cycling coach Sir Dave Brailsford, who popularized the notion of "Marginal Gains"—small, consistent improvements that lead to significant long-term success.

I remember meeting with my squadron commander, LCol Lawrence. LCol Lawrence is a strong advocate for the 12 Wing innovation program. During our meeting, he paused as we discussed a suggestion from the program. A grin spread across his face as he said, "*Ah, the power of 1%.*"

Give People a Reason to Buy In

Building momentum is more effective than any other approach to removing resistance. Team members naturally embrace positive organizational changes when they see their colleagues being acknowledged for adopting new ideas.

💡 Lessons Learned

> 🛠 Minor improvements involve discovering fresh methods to organize your workspace, adjusting established procedures, and utilizing digital tools that enhance efficiency.

- ⚒ When you implement various small changes, they will gradually turn your situation into something substantial.
- ⚒ Every small step created through implementing the 1% Improvement Mindset represents value in advancement.
- ⚒ People should implement even modest ideas with determination because their regular execution leads to primary transformative results.

The lesson I want you to bring everywhere is this: micro-improvements yield enormous outcomes in life.

The Psychology of Ownership

The feeling you get from helping to construct something becomes a profound blend of pride and obligation regarding its overall success. When the psychology of ownership activates, this feeling arises within you. People involved in creating a project or process naturally become more supportive as they have invested time in its development. Human instincts, rather than mystical forces, drive this effect.

Let's break it down. You join a team that develops new ideas, where every member contributes their thoughts to shape the end product. Employees gain authority when they can integrate their ideas into an evolving design, which is evident in the finished product. Your empowerment occurs precisely at that moment since the project now belongs to you. Commitment to success grows because the idea no longer belongs to someone else but now exists as your creation.

The process of ownership alters how individuals approach everyday situations. It transforms people from passive decision recipients into active participants who contribute to developing their work environment. By engaging in project development, your brain automatically values the outcomes more, enhancing your dedication to their success.

🔑 Key Takeaways

- 🔒 Increased Commitment Starting new projects feels natural when support is present. You're less likely to abandon work that you're passionate about. Your pride in your work motivates you to put extra effort into creating an exceptional final product.
- 🔒 Enhanced Motivation: Taking ownership and receiving positive feedback boost motivation, especially as you commit more time and effort to projects. Successful contributions inspire continued contributions.
- 🔒 Better Problem Solving: Project commitment encourages you to tackle complex problems wherein you assume responsibility for its success and proactively solve issues rather than pass them off.
- 🔒 Stronger Team Dynamics: Taking ownership fosters team spirit whereby contributors enjoy a sense of shared achievement and

responsibility, workplace friendships, and a culture focused on common goals.

During the 12 Wing innovation process, we avoided top-down mandates. Our team involved people from all levels as we developed the process, starting with discussions and ending with MVPs and final tweaks. The outcome? Initial skeptics became enthusiastic supporters because they played a role in its creation.

The following key aspects surfaced after applying the principles of ownership.

◇ Empower Participation

All members should have opportunities to contribute, regardless of their position. Seeking suggestions from all staff will gather diverse viewpoints and foster a workplace culture that values each individual's input.

◇ Encourage Collaboration

Organizations enhance their agency through collaborative work. The partnership among team members working on an idea naturally fosters connectedness, resulting in mutual dedication. This collaborative process goes beyond merely dividing tasks, as members come together to create a shared vision to which they feel personally accountable.

◇ Create a Feedback Loop

A feedback loop should be established to demonstrate the impact of their implemented ideas. Regular feedback enables individuals to maintain their sense of ownership and shows how their work results in tangible outcomes.

Empowering people to take ownership is just the beginning. For that ownership to be meaningful, it must be supported by a culture of transparency— where trust is built through open communication, clear decision-making, and shared accountability.

Build Trust Through Transparency

Transparent processes foster trust among employees. When teams are open, members are more engaged in supporting changes. Involving team members early in the process is key to effective change. Successful social change requires more than top-down decisions; programs promoting employee involvement are crucial. Allowing staff to share ideas increases enthusiasm for new practices.

Encourage team ownership when facing challenges or starting projects. Employee engagement relies on two main strategies: holding sharing sessions for input and collaborating on projects. It's important for all team members to feel shared responsibility.

Real change comes from empowering individuals to lead and work together on solutions. This enhances problem-solving and strengthens commitment to the organization. Lasting positive change happens by giving people ownership.

Trust and transparency are key for teamwork. Teams need a flexible approach to turn ideas into action, which is where Agile project management helps. It allows organizations to quickly test solutions, adapt to challenges, and improve continuously. In military aviation, where precision is crucial, Agile principles help overcome red tape and drive change.

CHAPTER 3

AGILE PROJECT MANAGEMENT IN MILITARY INNOVATION

"It is not the strongest of the species that survive, nor the most intelligent, but the one most responsive to change."

CHARLES DARWIN

This chapter introduces agile project management as a strategic factor for military innovation, offering unexpected advantages. From a structured hierarchical environment perspective, the concept of agility may initially seem incompatible. However, this adaptable working pattern has proven transformational even within military operations.

The term 'agile' extends beyond the hype of the technology industry. The Agile mindset enables teams to respond swiftly and absorb feedback for continuous improvement. 12 Wing adopted a new approach by moving away from the expectation of flawless solutions without effort from below. Our strategy involved addressing emerging issues through controlled and intentional small steps.

The upcoming section employs agile principles to illustrate how our team tackled complex field challenges. Initially, we broke down extensive issues into manageable component tasks that could be completed efficiently. We developed Minimum Viable Products (MVPs) as basic operational versions of concepts to test and refine progressively until the concepts evolved into their final applications.

This method fostered swift decision-making and empowered team members for experimental and innovative work. Whenever mistakes happened, agile projects became growth opportunities, while each project's success represented progress toward more efficient operations.

Throughout this chapter, we will explore the agile project management revolution, which has modern-ized innovation within a system that once adhered to rigid protocols. Key elements include risk-taking, flexibility, and the essential role of learning at each interval. The subsequent discussion will demonstrate how several compact, agile movements yield substan-tial innovations for military purposes.

Limits of Structured Environments

Traditional techniques commonly fail to deliver results in an environment where structure dominates operations. A long-running organization with established organizational hierarchies maintains many procedures that have endured for decades. These proven techniques delivered successful results earlier, but the evolving industry landscape makes them inadequate for modern needs. The following section contains practical examples that illustrate my point.

Stuck in a Rigid Mold

Let's examine the following fictitious example:

Sky Aero, a long-established aircraft component manufacturer, still uses the same methods it has for years. The company relies on traditional paper-based practices, including manual checklists, paper documents, and strict procedures. At first, this appears to be a dependable system. Sticking to old methods may seem safer than making changes.

The main downside arises when new challenges surface, as the rigid system can hinder decision-making. These challenges include unexpected shortages of critical parts or the need for technology adaptation.

An Example from the Field

When Cpl Evan Angelo first introduced the idea for Wing Mental Health Day, it faced predictable skepticism. Some managers viewed it as an unnecessary break in operations, questioning whether it would genuinely improve workplace morale or just another well-intentioned initiative that would fade into obscurity. Others believed mental health was a personal responsibility, not an organizational priority, making structured awareness days seem overreach.

Yet, the first Wing Mental Health Day proved to be a turning point. Instead of disrupting productivity, it enhanced it by giving personnel space to discuss challenges, connect with peers, and access resources they might not have sought. Conversations that would have been brushed aside under the weight of daily responsibilities were now happening openly. Teams reported reduced stress, improved focus, and a stronger sense of support from leadership.

Rather than just a single event, Wing Mental Health Day became a catalyst for a broader cultural shift, where prioritizing well-being wasn't a distraction but a necessity. The resistance it initially faced reminded us that change often feels inconvenient until its benefits become undeniable. Organizations don't just improve morale by embracing small, structured initiatives like this. Still, they build a workplace where people feel valued, heard, and empowered to bring their best selves to the mission daily.

The Challenge of Hierarchical Decision-Making

In traditional settings, decision-making can be limited. Often, only senior leaders have the authority to make decisions, and they must pass orders through various levels of hierarchy. This method is effective for routine tasks but slows the ability to adapt quickly to changes.

A team in the field spots a problem and suggests a potential fix. However, in a traditional organization, the solution must be approved by multiple layers of management. Long waiting times can be frustrating and might result in missed opportunities.

Inflexibility in Changing Times

Rapid changes in the world's landscape arise from new technological advancements, evolving operational methods, and frequently occurring emerging challenges. Conventional techniques often move slowly in adopting innovative approaches. These systems are based on the belief that traditional practices represent the best operations. When individuals cling to this mindset, responding to new information and unforeseen challenges becomes difficult.

Consider the case of manufacturing operations to illustrate my point. Factories operated on scheduled production alongside inflexible workflow systems. They encountered difficulties when market requirements transformed, or new business competition emerged because their operational systems lacked adequate adaptability. Lean manufacturing arose as an organizational response, as its principles focus on continuous process enhancement and the ability to adjust to changes, starkly contrasting conventional rigid systems.

Bottomup BREAKTHROUGH

❓ Why It Matters

So, why does all this matter? Traditional approaches fail to fully reveal their weaknesses until organizations realize their inability to respond to emerging challenges due to rigid processes. These processes become obstacles to creativity, resulting in slowed development when strict limitations are imposed. Organizational procedures hinder introducing transformational ideas that could lead to substantial improvements.

The established methods at 12 Wing created barriers to rapid process enhancements and technology adoption. A significant change occurred after we began questioning long-standing practices and experimenting with alternative approaches. Our challenge to conventional methods and our move away from rigid processes created new opportunities for innovation.

🗣 Practical Advice

- ☑ Question the Status Quo: You should question existing practices simply because they have remained unchanged. Verify whether current procedures are the best option for success.
- ☑ Encourage Experimentation Develop implementation methods for limited experimentation or trial runs. These systems can evaluate new ideas before making changes on a larger scale. A digital solution should be

rolled out in a smaller setting to ascertain whether it addresses issues more effectively than traditional procedures.

☑ Foster Open Communication Every organization member must be able to express themselves, especially staff who interact directly with the affected processes. Employees at the forefront understand the solutions, which leads to the discovery of innovative work methods.

☑ Be Open to Change Recognize that the global landscape demands updated approaches that result in enhanced processes. Organizations must consistently refine their core principles to stay competitive and effective.

☑ Learn from Other Industries When I arrived at PQ, Diane asked me to look at successful practices from non-military organizations. She said that using effective methods from others can improve our efficiency. Innovative ideas to enhance your business can come from anywhere, regardless of your industry.

Traditional methods can cause inefficiency and hinder innovation in everyday operations. Organizations should acknowledge these drawbacks and look for solutions that promote real improvements.

To enhance systems, it's often necessary to test established practices. Even minor changes to a process can yield significant results, as continuous innovation relies on these tweaks. By moving past traditional limitations, you can embrace a flexible mindset that encourages constantly exploring new ways to improve.

Implementing Agile with Limited Resources: A Lean Approach

The innovation program at 12 Wing started without funding or dedicated personnel. We only had a group of passionate volunteers and a clear direction to create an enhanced work environment that functioned more efficiently and intelligently. The question remained regarding how to reach our objective since we did not have new funding or dedicated unique resources.

Implementing Agile principles became the solution to our problems. Agile represents a specific working methodology focusing on minimalistic steps, quick achievements, and ongoing improvement initiatives. We began executing immediately to generate measured improvements through trial and error learning.

One of the best examples of bottom-up innovation at 12 Wing came from Cpl Pierre Lacombe. Pierre recognized the challenges of retrieving mission-critical data in real-time, especially in low-connectivity environments, so he designed the TIMS Recce App. This lightweight, adaptable solution streamlined intelligence gathering.

Unlike rigid software solutions that are developed from the top down, TIMS developed naturally from actual operational needs. It was created as a set of

HTML files that anyone could easily change with a simple text editor, allowing users to customize the system to fit their needs. Instead of waiting for a perfect finished product, Cpl Lacombe and his team released a simple version (Build 2.0.1) and quickly made improvements based on user feedback.

Agile methodology fosters an exploratory culture in organizations where finding perfect solutions right away isn't necessary. The process involves a few initial operations, followed by testing, gathering feedback, and several rounds of improvements until success is reached. This approach helped us fix problems early, avoiding costly mistakes and allowing for quick solutions.

Agile within a structured workplace

The program started with simple, innovative projects to show quick, measurable benefits and build trust. This approach led to clear improvements instead of complicated plans. These visible benefits helped to eliminate doubts about the project and encouraged enthusiasm.

We kept our methods straightforward and effective by avoiding complex planning and lengthy proposals. We focused on easy ideas that delivered immediate results, quickly demonstrating their value to the organization, which built mutual trust and sustained momentum.

The team provided ongoing feedback using accessible tools and processes during each project phase. Their direct and factual reporting from their work environment ensured the solutions were effective in real operations.

The key principle of Agile emphasizes teamwork instead of rigid hierarchies. People at every level had many chances to share their skills and ideas in all meetings. Our organization encouraged open discussions, which improved solution development and gained full employee support.

We recognized that small mistakes might happen with Agile practices, but these valuable learning moments led to improvements. Our team viewed each setback as a step towards successfully making the final solution work.

My recommendation to implement Agile principles in your organization follows these points:

- Your projects will succeed more effectively with a limited startup size, regular testing, and prompt adaptations.
- Encourage each team member to share their suggestions and take ownership of their work.
- To build trust, it helps to focus on visible, tangible improvements that everyone can recognize.
- Learn from mistakes, as avoiding errors altogether results in no progress.

The introduction of Agile methodology at 12 Wing demonstrated that innovative solutions can exist without elaborate costs. Our organization showed great success through employee empowerment while making minor improvements, which led to continuous development regardless of limited resources.

Rapid Prototyping and Minimal Viable Products (MVPs)

The MVP approach encourages businesses to create their most basic solution rather than spending excessive time on perfect answers. Users should be able to test an MVP prototype since its core functions allow for quick feedback collection.

Consider the process of building a vehicle. The construction begins with something other than a premium sports car model. The initial step would be to start with the simplest version possible: a skateboard. This basic version lacks complete features and does not have wheels. Users can see and interact with the tangible reality of this version. After using the product, our users will provide feedback on the necessary features.

User feedback is essential for adding wheels to the skateboard, which eventually becomes a scooter. At each development stage, users provide input on whether their needs are being met. The basic skateboard changes into a bicycle, then a motorcycle, and finally evolves into a car.

Using the MVP approach, organizations change their product development process. Users guide you in meeting their needs step by step.

The Power of Rapid Prototyping

Rapid prototyping is key to MVP thinking. It replaces long planning and detailed building of potentially unsuitable solutions, allowing users to create simple prototypes to test their ideas quickly. This process focuses on sensitivity and adaptability, as faster product development leads to quicker results and program success.

At 12 Wing, we use this approach daily. When Sgt Staci Foster proposed a Women in Aviation Event, it was more than just another tour; it aimed to change perceptions and create opportunities. The idea was simple: invite female maintainers, aircrew, and industry professionals to showcase aviation careers in the RCAF. She partnered with Elevate Aviation and Techsploration and contacted local aviation colleges and training institutes.

Instead of waiting for a complete plan, Staci took an Agile route. She informed her idea's approving authority, secured approval, and swiftly organized the first event for 2024.

The Value of Feedback

When I was involved with maintenance planning at 12 Wing, I recall sitting in a meeting where a new planning tool was introduced. After listening to the proposed benefits, I asked a straightforward question: "Did you consult with maintenance planners while developing this tool?" The response... No.

Failing to request or Ignoring user feedback can lead organizations to face negative consequences, and I've witnessed this firsthand. Often, people present shiny new digital tools with pride after investing significant time into them. They might say, "Check this out! Isn't it amazing?"

However, upon closer examination, these tools, despite their impressive designs, frequently fail when in use. Why? Users were not involved early enough in the development process. The creators built their products without validating user requirements through testing. The result? While the tool appeared great, users found it difficult to use because it lacked intuitiveness. I learned that even brilliant ideas can falter if users don't grasp their value or how to integrate them into their daily activities.

Real-World Example: Junior Leadership Handbook

Taking on a leadership role brings challenges, from addressing grievances to aiding subordinates with personal struggles, yet many junior leaders at 12 Wing lacked a structured guide. Rather than awaiting top-down solutions, MCpl Matthew Gillard proposed the Junior Leadership Handbook. This concise and practical resource details essential contacts, recommended courses, and step-by-step guidance for navigating leadership scenarios. After discussions with CWO Wezenbeek, the idea gained approval, and development began with direct input from those who would benefit most.

Like many bottom-up innovations, this initiative started small but with a clear purpose—to empower leaders with the tools they needed to succeed. Instead of complex policies or lengthy courses, the handbook offered quick, actionable insights, making leadership development more accessible. It was a straightforward but high-impact fix to a widespread challenge, proving that sometimes the most effective innovations aren't about technology but people helping people.

❓ Why MVP Thinking Matters

MVP thinking functions effectively in software systems and technology development, policy-making strategies, and procedural frameworks. It demonstrates its efficacy across all areas that require valuable solutions, including policy formulation and procedural definitions. Why? Practicality takes precedence over theoretical excellence through MVP thinking.

Our team gained substantial advantages, which include:

◇ Quick Wins Build Momentum

Achieving small accomplishments boosts confidence, which makes everyone enthusiastic about their work. Employees who witness quick successes in their tasks continue to feel motivated to share new ideas.

◇ Early Feedback Saves Resources

Testing your ideas early allows you to identify problems before their consequences become significant. Finding immediate solutions helps organizations eliminate errors before committing substantial time and resources to ineffective strategies.

◇ Solutions, Not Just Theories

Every modification you make reflects user requirements and brings value to the real world.

4 Ways for Successfully Using MVPs and Rapid Prototyping

My advice to those planning MVP and rapid prototyping implementation in their organizations includes these key points:

1. Start Simple

Avoid aiming for a perfect solution right away. Start by building a basic version of your concept that will serve as a test and gather essential insights.

2. Collect Feedback

Begin collecting user feedback as soon as the first basic version is implemented, and continue conducting regular user surveys. Users should provide feedback through ongoing check-ins. Adjust your approach based on user feedback you gather by listening to their comments.

3. Stay Flexible

Adjustments to your approach must be made while the project is in progress. The key purpose behind rapid prototyping and MVP development is to learn and swiftly adapt the strategy.

4. Keep Everyone Informed

Your team needs regular updates on the information you've acquired and how you're adjusting your approach. This approach ensures that people stay engaged and motivated because information is shared openly.

💡 Lessons Learned

- **Test Early, Test Often:** Early and ongoing testing prevents investing resources in problems that can be avoided.
- **Define Success via Users:** Establish realistic KPIs to assess whether your MVP is achieving intended outcomes, your capacity to anticipate project success secondary to user concept perceptions; monitoring feedback and responding promptly is crucial.
- **Iterate, Don't Over-Engineer:** Rather than immediately seek out a perfect solution, create simple ones and improve the product per user feedback (repeating as necessary).

Bringing It All Together

Humility is a central principle of the MVP mindset, as every concept development begins with the full recognition that you are unsure of everything. The initial quality of even the best innovations is imperfect immediately after their release. These systems evolve gradually as they acquire knowledge through continuous development and adaptation to new information.

Adopting MVPs and rapid prototyping at 12 Wing has led to an organizational transformation. Implementing MVPs allows us to build functional solutions efficiently, improve everyday processes, and establish a culture of ongoing progress.

The path to innovation success does not rely on massive, complex solutions. Simple concepts that undergo testing, refinement, and scaling yield the most significant results.

Project success can be achieved by selecting small initiatives, conducting regular testing, and treating each iteration as a learning opportunity. MVP thinking fosters rapid transformation that is easily observable by anyone.

Gathering User Feedback: The Iterative Innovation Cycle

The key element driving true innovation success is user feedback. Here's the secret: it's all about user feedback. Collecting input from users is crucial for developing successful innovations. Listening closely to those who use our solutions daily has proven the most effective method for creating excellent solutions at 12 Wing Shearwater.

❓ Why Feedback is Essential

When developing a business strategy, you should seek feedback from stakeholders and team members before finalizing your approach. Their insights can help you adapt and improve your methods in future initiatives. Business innovation works similarly. Without proper feedback, you may create solutions that aren't needed, which is likely when user feedback is left out of the process, leading to wasted time and resources.

The Iterative Innovation Cycle Explained

At 12 Wing, we embraced a rapid launch strategy focused on quick iterations to achieve our goals. We prioritized swift deployment by introducing an initial version as our Minimum Viable Product, understanding that some mistakes would inevitably arise in the early stages. This approach allowed us to gather valuable user feedback right away.

We actively sought insights from our peers, using their experiences to identify flaws and areas for improvement. This feedback loop highlighted our initial missteps and equipped us with the knowledge to address these issues efficiently during the development phase.

Our early launch and responsiveness to feedback demonstrated that even minor actions can drive meaningful cultural shifts, paving the way for continuous enhancement of our processes and workplace environment.

Collecting Feedback Effectively

Once you've completed your first version of the work, gather feedback from others. Here are some effective methods:

⬦ At 12 Wing, staff used simple strategies to collect feedback successfully. Technicians using the new system should engage in direct conversations to ask about the system's performance and areas for improvement. When respondents felt comfortable, they shared honest and straightforward feedback.

⬦ The Microsoft Forms platform enabled quick online surveys, allowing everyone, including the more reserved, to share their opinions safely from their computers. 12 Wing also hosted public sessions known as Town Hall Sessions, which allowed team members to provide constructive input while fostering trust and transparency.

The Iterative Innovation Cycle in Action

A fundamental component behind this operation is called the Iterative Innovation Cycle. Sounds technical. But it's pretty simple:

- The first step involves developing essential solutions from existing issues for testing purposes.
- The solution should be accessible for employees to try during regular work activities.

- Users should provide their perspectives, including both positive and negative feedback regarding their experiences.
- The feedback received should guide the enhancement and perfection of existing solutions.
- Continuous refinement of the concept must occur until the solution becomes effective for its intended purpose.

The Iterative Innovation Cycle is a process of constant improvement where solutions are created from real-life problems, tested in regular work settings, updated based on user input, and repeatedly improved until they work effectively.

💡 **Lessons Learned**

- ⚒ Repeated check-ins provide better insight than lengthy assessments. As innovation without active user input bred guesstimations at 12 Wing, continuous feedback (rather) gave us the wherewithal to develop effective solutions and drive progress.
- ⚒ Trust and engagement grow when feedback drives tangible action. Employees must feel safe to express ideas and know their input is valued; project iterations incorporating feedback form a culture where engaged people drive change.
- ⚒ Innovation thrives when teams actively listen and adapt. By integrating user feedback,

teams naturally drive innovation forward, fostering a continuous improvement cycle.

Measuring Success with Data

To truly innovate, we must develop and implement new ideas using current data. Collecting actual data from various sources helps us measure our performance. Without measuring our impact, knowing if we've succeeded is difficult.

At 12 Wing, everyone learned that success requires more than personal effort; it's about tracking our progress effectively. There are straightforward ways to measure our success that can lead to positive insights. The measurement process involves gathering key data points in their simplest form to show how effective our changes are.

❓ Why Current Data Matters

1. It Provides Proof of Impact

Data gives us hard evidence. Implementing a new process that accelerates maintenance duties requires evaluation. We avoid depending on personal opinions by monitoring the daily time savings achieved through our approaches. Identifying clear improvements in numbers indicates the path we are taking correctly.

2. It Helps Us Continuously Improve

The information we collect shows us both successful and unsuccessful outcomes. An idea's unsuccessful outcome allows us to modify it before additional testing. Success measurement operates beyond verification of correctness since its primary function supports development and enhancement in our ongoing work.

3. It Builds Credibility

Numbers speak louder than opinions. Clear, visible improvements in our work lead to increased trust from leadership teams, colleagues, and doubters. Actual advantages in the real world make people more inclined to back changes in operations.

How to Measure Success Effectively

Measuring success involves every person finding their preferred method. Several straightforward methods exist to acquire valuable information, which I will describe below.

Define What Success Looks Like

In project management, we emphasize the importance of creating a metric for the '**Definition of Done**'. This helps team members know when a task is complete. Establishing clear metrics is essential to measuring success. Think about what achievement you want to measure: Are you looking to save time, reduce errors, or enhance efficiency? Your goals will guide your data monitoring.

Basic Tracking Tools Should Be Used to Follow Progress

- Valuable data collection does not require advanced software tools. Simple, accessible tools are the most potent data-tracking instruments.
- Microsoft and Google Forms allow users to conduct rapid feedback collection surveys.
- Excel and Google Sheets are essential data collection tools to document the time effectiveness, process optimization, and error elimination results.
- Simple checklists with logs serve as convenient methods to track daily operational Progress.

Get Regular Feedback from Users

Statistics alone don't provide the full picture. We need to combine performance data with insights from the system operators.

- Leadership should initiate interactive team assembly sessions to gather helpful input.
- Your users will give sincere feedback through confidential survey questions.
- Users should be monitored for consistent evaluation of workflow improvement due to the implemented changes.

Make the Data Visible

People can readily choose to disregard information when they cannot observe data. Presenting results helps generate team enthusiasm and attracts more team involvement.

- Show ongoing process updates in accessible areas for all staff members.
- Before-and-after visuals should be presented to illustrate transformational results.
- Small process successes should be acknowledged by demonstrating how the 10-minute reduction in shift time translates into longer durations for the broader picture.

Adjust and Improve Based on What You Learn

The value of data extends beyond confirming achievements because it helps organizations achieve constant enhancement. Any idea that fails to achieve results leads to adaptation and additional attempts to make it work.

When results fall short of expectations, it's essential to identify the reasons for failure and make necessary adjustments. Feedback on modifications or new features provides clear implementation criteria, while continuous small refinements over time lead to significant improvements.

💡 Lessons Learned

🔨 Accurate measurement drives real improvement. Tracking the right performance indicators, not just data, ensures that changes lead to meaningful progress. Without proper measurement, improvements remain guess-work.

🔨 Start with what you have, basic data and direct feedback. Sophisticated tools aren't required to monitor performance. Combining simple tracking with user insights often provides the most valuable results.

🔨 Sharing real results builds trust and support. Transparency in data fosters engagement as people rally behind proven successes rather than assumptions.

🔨 Tracking, testing, and refining fuel continuous innovation. Measured adjustments create a learning cycle that leads to sustained progress and breakthrough solutions.

Data collection is just the start. To drive real improvements, we must find the symptoms and the root causes of problems. Root Cause Analysis (RCA) reveals true inefficiencies for lasting solutions. Next, we'll see how RCA helped 12 Wing achieve breakthroughs and how you can use it to create organizational change.

CHAPTER 4

THE POWER OF ROOT CAUSE ANALYSIS

"A problem well stated is a problem half solved."

CHARLES KETTERING

The 5 Whys technique was originally developed by Sakichi Toyoda, the founder of Toyota Industries, in the early 20th century. It became a core problem-solving method within the Toyota Production System and was later widely adopted in Lean Manufacturing and Six Sigma methodologies.

What are the 5 Whys? My first experience with the 5 Whys occurred when Nick and I met with Col Holmes and CWO Wezenbeek to present the 12 Wings Innovation Charter. Nick suggested I present the completed Charter to the Wing Commander for approval. As I presented the details of the Charter, I noticed a peculiar interaction between Col Holmes and me. Typically, you expect someone to ask why if they seek clarification, however... I would present a concept from the Charter, and Col. Holmes would ask "Why," I would elaborate and then ask again, "Why." This sequence happened five times. As I finished elaborating, I noticed a smile across Homer's face; I glanced at CWO Wezenbeek and Nick to see if I had overlooked something. Then, Col. Holmes explained that asking why five times allows you to get to the **root cause** of a problem. It instantly clicked, like a light went on in my head.

The root cause analysis process requires no complicated theoretical concepts or sophisticated equipment. Our commitment to examining the initial symptoms is essential to uncovering the core reason behind the issues. Managing garden weeds is akin to this process since merely trimming leaves won't stop the weeds from regrowing. Addressing the root of the issue and extracting it can resolve the problem permanently.

This chapter illustrates our use of root cause analysis to tackle real problems at 12 Wing, leading to enduring solutions and significant advancements. The lesson will equip you with practical methods to identify fundamental causes while allowing your work to remain free from common errors, ensuring your solutions effectively resolve issues rather than offering temporary fixes.

The following material discusses asking the right questions and developing lasting solutions. Let's dive in!

The solution lies in five "why" questions that uncover genuine problem origins. The simplest yet most effective question you can ask to find answers is "Why?" Most people think they fully understand all aspects of a problem, even though they often encounter it. People typically address superficial issues with fixes instead of investigating the underlying causes. The Five Whys method provides a structured approach to identify root problems effectively. Repeated use of "Why?" for five rounds helps you uncover the true base causes behind challenges.

❓ Why the Five Whys Matter

While the Five Whys technique is essential, it stands out as an effective method for problem-solving. Each time you ask "Why?" the investigation delves deeper to uncover the true source of the problem for both you and your team.

A lingering suspension of maintenance activities might occupy your thoughts. You might typically conclude that the technician lacks the necessary parts to carry out their tasks. While this answer holds, what underpins that omission?

Your inquiry must persist in exploring the reasons behind the issues until you uncover that Canada is the aircraft's only customer, leading to global supply chain challenges. The core solution becomes evident: the issue extends beyond ordering parts on time. The supply chain system is grappling with a significant problem that quick, temporary fixes cannot resolve.

The real cause surfaces at this stage of the investigation.

A Closer Look: The Five Whys in Action

Remember, you don't always need to ask why exactly five times; you can reach the root cause much sooner. Let me explain:

Why is there a delay?

- The technician team lacks appropriate parts for their work.
- The technicians lack the necessary components that comprise their work equipment.
- For this reason, the system does not stock parts.

Why aren't they stocked?

A parts-on-demand supply chain receives real-time requests for necessary components from a supply system. This system ensures that essential parts are delivered efficiently, matching the specific production needs without excess inventory.

Why does the supply mechanism operate on a demand basis?

Canada is the exclusive customer of the Cyclone, which hinders bulk purchasing operations.

Bottomup BREAKTHROUGH

❓ Why This Matters

The supply chain is limited because Canada is the only market for Cyclone aircraft products, making it difficult to create worldwide distribution systems.

The main issue is that the parts supply network only serves the specific aircraft model purchased. We can explore alternatives like different supply agreements and new ways of producing parts to solve this. Making urgent part orders when inventory runs out won't fix the core problem; it only deals with the symptoms.

🧩 Piecing It Together

Solving complex challenges is like putting together a puzzle. Initially, the pieces may seem unrelated, so we focus on the obvious ones—the symptoms. However, just as you can't force puzzle pieces together, quick fixes won't resolve deeper problems. The solution lies in spotting patterns and understanding how each piece connects to the whole. Similarly, effective problem-solving involves looking beyond symptoms to identify root causes. This leads us to the important task of finding the fundamental issues behind our challenges.

Most Problems Have Deeper Causes

The apparent symptoms create a strong desire to address them. However, surface-level corrections cannot eliminate underlying issues because the crucial problems remain undetectable. For example, you can remove garden weeds through leaf trimming, yet roots will remain because leaves do not help eliminate the original cause. Destroying the foundation is necessary to eliminate the problem permanently.

🗣 Practical Advice

☑ Be cautious when evaluating whether you have found and addressed the original problem. Does this symptom exist for a specific original reason?

The Five Whys Forces Clarity

Repeating the question "Why?" can make your initial assumptions unstable. Demanding additional parts would not fix the fundamental problem when the root causes stem from a supply system incapable of supporting stocking; by repeatedly repeating the question "Why?" you can achieve the best possible logical explanation at your base level.

Continue questioning with "**Why**" even if your response starts with the second or third "Why." Continue questioning the cause to ensure that you identify all fundamental underlying problems.

Great Leaders Ask Better Questions

I was surprised when Col Holmes asked many questions during our meetings. The Value Handling experts explained that they wanted to find important issues instead of questioning my reasoning. The leaders at 12 Wing used the Five Whys technique to help me improve my argument and find real solutions.

Bottomup BREAKTHROUGH

👤 Practical Advice

☑ If you pose in-depth questions exploring the underlying issues, your team will identify their roots. This approach empowers team members to apply critical thinking instead of relying on immediate solutions.

🛠 Practical Tip

◇ Gather the Right People

Those who experience the problem firsthand possess the most specific knowledge; thus, they must participate in problem-solving. Team members' insights result in the most precise answers.

◇ Stay Focused on the Process

Check each answer to ensure it responds to the previous question, starting with "Why?" Unrelated digressions happen occasionally.

◇ Use Simple Language

You don't need fancy terms. This helps to promote honest answers in plain talk. The point is to cause people to dig deep rather than espouse jargon.

◇ Document As You Go

You may not see how fast you are improving. Each time you ask "Why?" and write down the answers, it makes things clearer and easier to look back on later.

Identify the Main Cause and Stop.

You can ask "Why?" three or four times, or even more if needed. This is just a guideline. If you find an underlying issue that explains the problem, stop there.

A Mindset for Innovation

Since discovering its value for 12 Wing's challenges, I've used the Five Whys countless times. Every time, it reminds me that real innovation is not a band-aid over the symptom but finding and fixing why the symptom exists. The result has been more effective and long-lasting solutions that save time, resources, and frustration in the long run.

💡 **Lessons Learned**

- Institutional settings, including the military, encourage individuals to accept basic responses. In contrast, a commitment to asking "Why" pinpoints real issues and fosters innovation.
- The Five Whys tackle current and prevent future problems, asking questions and digging deeper to uncover the root cause of obstacles and thus unearth effective solutions.
- This practice promotes sustainable methods to achieve lasting benefits, mitigating issues now and in the future. Your organization, likewise, encourages meaningful growth via deep analysis rather than superficial thinking.

Fixing Symptoms vs. Addressing the Root Cause

In a meeting with CWO Wezenbeek, we discussed creating new employee awards. While this idea seems beneficial because people appreciate being recognized, it only addresses a symptom of deeper problems rather than solving the actual issues at hand.

The Proposal: More Technician Awards

The proposal originated from Master Warrant Officer (MWO) Hatfield, who has since been promoted to Chief Warrant Officer (CWO). CWO Hatfield suggested implementing special recognition awards exclusively for technicians. The reasoning behind this proposal appeared well-founded: technicians diligently worked many hours but lacked adequate opportunities to receive recognition for their efforts.

The Wing Chief, CWO Wezenbeek, had agreed to be the Approving Authority for this endeavour. Consequently, the Wing Chief met with his Squadron Chiefs to discuss the merits of this proposal. When I met with the Wing Chief to discuss the idea, he stated, "*Multiple squadron chiefs informed me we already had sufficient awards for technicians.*" I paused and contemplated my response.

Our existing award system seemed adequate, so why did CWO Hatfield believe more awards were needed?

The root issue required further investigation

The feedback inspired me to dig deeper, so I initiated an investigation. My research began by checking all actual locations of the current awards documentation, digital or otherwise.

I thoroughly audited every Squadron's SharePoint page to confirm whether the available awards were listed and found that no site included the mentioned awards. At the end of my investigation, I noted all the awards documentation was hidden in an annex on a section of the Wing Chief's SharePoint page. In other words

The **root** appeared that members could not easily access all the information about existing awards and nomination processes from a central location. Wing members found the nomination process difficult to understand due to its historical context. People felt there was a need for more awards because the current ones were often overlooked. However, a shortage of awards never existed; the main issue was unclear processes and limited accessibility.

The Real Solution: Accessibility, Not More Awards

We recognized that the root issue was the combination of bad visibility and a complex nomination process, so we created a simple solution to address the root.

Here's what we created:

◇ A Digital Solution

The team created a Microsoft Form that replicated the functionalities present in the 12 Wing Ideas Portal. A few clicks allowed people to nominate colleagues because they could avoid completing extensive paperwork requirements. The simplified process became more user-friendly and more inviting to the system users.

◇ A Streamlined Workflow

When personnel submitted their nominations, the assistant serving under the Wing Chief automatically received notification through email. After receiving a nomination, the assistant provided the requirements and followed up so employees avoided operating in bureaucratic mystery.

◇ Improved Awareness & Visibility

The base staff installed QR code posters throughout the facility, and visitors needed only to use their phone cameras to open the nomination form.

- We positioned the dedicated link beside Ideas Team on 12 Wing's main SharePoint page, making it highly visible.
- The SharePoint homepage gained maximum visibility from our designed banner advertisement.

- The more straightforward access to awards eliminated the initial problem that warrants new ones in the first place.

💡 Lessons Learned

🔨 **Clarity Regarding Awards:** Beyond new awards, the core issue is deficient access to existing award information. In addressing the underlying problem, we recognize many feel overlooked due to inadequate nomination processes and a lack of awareness; disseminating content can resolve this issue.

🔨 **Information Accessibility:** Resources unknown to people are non-existent; efforts to simplify information system navigation are more effective than promoting complex programs (e.g., new award systems).

Understanding the issue is only the first step—now, let's explore practical strategies to ensure recognition systems are accessible, fair, and truly impactful.

🗣 Practical Advice

☑ Review the Current Process: Start by examining how operations work now. Those requesting new awards should check the existing process to ensure it meets their needs. Find out about the nomination procedure and assess whether the information is easily accessible.

☑ Relying on one opinion for important decisions is unwise. Squadron chiefs agreed with the Wing Chief that current awards provide sufficient recognition. Checking my SharePoint and speaking to squadron leaders clarified the situation.

☑ Users need quick access to nomination forms and sign-up sheets. The system should be accessible and clearly presented for user acceptance.

☑ Monitor and improve the new digital form by gathering feedback on accessibility after each use.

☑ Communicate the Change Every fix of a fundamental issue needs to be public knowledge. Increasing awareness helps eliminate persistent incorrect beliefs within the organization.

❓ Why It All Matters

Focusing on the right problem helps avoid widespread distress and wasted resources. Creating more awards would have complicated the system without solving the main issue. We looked at the situation from a wide perspective to ensure our solution would lead to lasting results.

The main problem shows that solving symptoms instead of fundamental issues leads to poor solutions. While symptoms are easy to see, we often miss other important aspects that define the problem. Quick fixes may seem easy, but they often lead to the original issue returning soon after. When organizations focus on the core issue, they can achieve real and lasting improvement.

People working in structured fields, like the military, should avoid quick solutions that appear simpler in the short term. Real strength lies in looking deeper to find the true root causes of problems. We found a solution that was easier than expected because we needed better ways to find and share information about existing awards, not more.

Before tackling new challenges or basic suggestions, take a moment to reflect. Ask yourself if the solution addresses the root cause or just the symptoms. By consistently practicing this thoughtful evaluation approach, you will discover powerful solutions.

Case Study: How a Simple Change Improved Efficiency

Allow me to explain how a simple adjustment greatly affected efficiency. The following story illustrates that making one crucial change can enhance efficiency. The following example showed that basic modifications can produce remarkable results when addressing significant challenges.

The Problem: Wasted Time and Frustration

When I arrived at 12 Wing, the maintenance teams faced a constant problem. Technicians wasted too much time dealing with paper task cards, which was frustrating. Task cards are important because they give technicians clear instructions for aircraft maintenance. The current system is not efficient and needs improvement.

Technicians travel long distances as part of their daily routines. They start by accessing computer terminals to print task cards. After printing, they collect their cards from a specific area. Then, they get the necessary tools from another location.

This back-and-forth process takes a lot of time and uses up valuable resources. Technicians often spend more time moving around than doing actual maintenance work.

Identifying the Opportunity

Enter Cpl Evan Angelo. Evan's method involved digitizing task cards so technicians could access them on tablets. This basic concept had a driving force that enhanced its effectiveness: no more printing task cards, instant access from anywhere in the hangar, and immediate tool checkout without extra trips.

Testing the Idea

We established a small trial program shortly after that. During implementation, only several technicians tested the new digital system. People's initial reception was doubtful. Several people asked whether the new system would generate sufficient time-saving advantages. Users immediately recognized the value of the digital cards after using them. The technicians reduced their physical movement to get around substantially, which boosted their performance levels.

Results: Small Change, Big Impact

Our data collection method was effective, and it quickly showed improvement. Technicians reduced their work time by 30 minutes to one hour each shift, saving many hours overall, totaling hundreds over the month. What started as a simple idea grew bigger than expected.

The success wasn't just about numbers; it also improved workplace morale. Technicians felt valued and appreciated. Staff noticed their concerns were taken seriously because their complaints were addressed directly.

Why Did This Work So Well?

The approach was effective because we digitized existing procedures rather than creating new ones. Technicians enhanced their efficiency immediately after implementing this system by increasing time efficiency. The solution was easy to adopt, requiring minimal time for each employee to grasp its operation.

🔑 Key Takeaway

🔒 Every little idea has the power to produce substantial effects. Wherever small steps are implemented, they produce big-scale outcomes across different teams.

Testing Matters:

Always start by testing your ideas on a small scale. Quick experiments help organizations spot issues that need fixing before implementing solutions more broadly. Frontline workers understand better than anyone what changes are needed in the operational system. Their feedback leads to meaningful solutions that provide real benefits. Improving business processes boosts morale, increases productivity, and enhances employee engagement.

This simple approach is a vital lesson in innovation. It shows that improvements can happen without major costs or drastic changes. By being open-minded and making small, smart adjustments, people can find important solutions right before them.

Avoid assuming that work inefficiency or frustration is inevitable. Instead, analyze small chances for adjustments that save you time, as this is more beneficial than considering large transformations. The time saved in small increments will create significant positive changes over the long run.

💡 Lessons Learned

- 📌 Every question requires a deeper analysis that goes beyond superficial responses. The most apparent issues often obscure deeper organizational challenges.
- 📌 You should question everything, as the initial answer may not reveal the truth. Insist on

examining all assumptions and encourage others to adopt the same mindset.

⚒ The direct involvement of individuals affected by the problem must be integral to the process. Those who experience the issue firsthand typically offer crucial insights into its true nature.

⚒ Your persistence will uncover the underlying issue, although it may take five "why" questions.

❓ Why It Matters

Implementing root cause analysis within 12 Wing established a solution-focused culture that enables personnel to find profound answers to organizational problems. Through our different approaches, we established preventive solutions that made the recurrence of these issues impossible.

We transformed our reactive behaviour into proactive improvement through our habitual questioning method. The changes in work processes, resource savings, and higher morale resulted in significant efficiency improvements.

Always mentally resist the urge to solve problems temporarily during your subsequent workplace issues. Your first objective must be to determine the actual reason behind this situation. Then, ask again—and again, up to five times if needed. Exposure to the underlying reasons leads to permanent solutions.

Making Root Cause Thinking a Habit

The recurrence of specific problems, despite your numerous attempts to resolve them, should spark your curiosity. You are not alone; many others confirm this truth through their head movements. I have often noticed within 12 Wing that issues that vanished one day reappeared the following week, frustrating team members. For this reason, we embraced root-cause thinking as a regular practice. I will outline the steps necessary to cultivate this habit in your personal or professional environment.

❓ Why Habits Matter

Consider brushing your teeth. Our brains follow this process automatically because we've learned it over time. The root cause thinking method operates on the same logical model. By incorporating this habit into your routine, you will naturally identify the underlying causes of your problems. This practice helps you resolve issues with lasting solutions and improved outcomes.

Turning Root Cause Analysis into a Habit: 5 Key Steps

The process of turning root-cause thinking into an automatic skill at 12 Wing can be learned through this approach:

1. Always Ask "Why?"

Start each troubleshooting process by asking yourself, "Why?" Does a problem truly exist? Repeat this question numerous times to uncover the actual source of the issue. Make this practice a daily habit when encountering minor problems to become more comfortable with the steps.

2. Make it a Team Effort

The root cause analysis process must include participation from multiple team members. Collaboration among coworkers and team members fosters a better understanding of specific problems. To enhance team questioning, encourage your colleagues to analyze problems collectively. Group interactions streamline the process of uncovering fundamental causes.

3. Keep it Simple and Accessible

Root cause analysis can deter people because they often view it as complex. However, it doesn't need to be. Implement clear communication strategies and straightforward, step-by-step approaches that people can easily follow. The personnel at 12 Wing used the Five Whys method and simple diagrams drawn on whiteboards or flip charts.

4. Make It Visible

Immediately upon discovery, root cause findings must be widely disseminated. The real solutions to problems must be visible throughout the workplace so everyone can see the benefits of daily work. The recommendations include posting research conclusions on bulletin boards, team pages, and SharePoint sites. When analysis succeeds, it generates positive results that encourage others to implement. The practice.

5. Regular Check-Ins

Meetings should be organized regularly to review problems and their root causes. When done consistently, this reinforces the behaviour while ensuring team members' responsibility to report root causes. A brief meeting held weekly will yield significant benefits. The primary focus of these sessions should be on learning and solutions rather than blaming or unconstructive criticism.

🛠 Practical Tip

Share positive outcomes widely. Recognition strengthens desirable team practices while motivating members to achieve even more profound levels of analysis.

💡 Lessons Learned

- 🔨 The Five Whys technique becomes more familiar when people repeat its use regularly. Staff members will naturally implement root-cause thinking before becoming aware of its occurrence.
- 🔨 Root cause analysis establishes itself as an organizational habit that changes your

cultural environment. People now avoid temporary answers so they can pursue sustainable resolutions.

Leadership sets a powerful tone by continuously using root-cause thinking. The leader's proactive attitude creates an instant transformation within their teams, which drives them to focus on practical solutions.

Root-cause thinking is a mindset shift that goes beyond solving problems. Organizations can prevent recurring challenges by addressing the real causes of issues and making lasting improvements.

Identifying the root cause is the beginning; the next step is taking action. How can we turn insights into real, sustainable innovation? That's where The Innovation Pathway comes in. In the next chapter, we'll look at how to move from recognizing problems to implementing effective, scalable solutions that create meaningful change.

CHAPTER 5

THE INNOVATION PATHWAY – FROM IDEA TO EXECUTION

"Vision without execution is hallucination."

THOMAS EDISON

When you have a brilliant idea and strong enthusiasm, they often fade if you can't bring them to fruition. You're not alone. The many great ideas at 12 Wing require a clear path and concrete implementation steps to flourish.

This chapter introduces the method that helped transform our initial ideas into completed innovations. This process will assist you in developing new concepts, garnering support from those around you, and overcoming challenges, allowing you to turn abstract ideas into tangible results.

The following text outlines strategies that empower anyone working within established organizations, teams, or independently to translate their visions into concrete actions.

The Idea Submission Process: Making Innovation Accessible to All

Do you remember seeing an excellent concept disappear amid standard procedures? The typical experience in large organizations shows how someone develops an innovative solution to a problem and then informs their leader, but the idea fades into obscurity. When we launched our innovation program, our goal at 12 Wing was to prevent such situations. We believed every concept deserves recognition, so we aimed to create a transparent, straightforward submission system available to all personnel.

At 12 Wing, we organized our innovation pipeline into six key phases: Ideation, Evaluation, Development, Presentation, Implementation, and Feedback. This structured approach ensured that ideas weren't merely submitted and forgotten—they were actively refined, tested, and executed with intention.

Ideation – The process begins when a staff member submits an idea, referred to internally as an 'Originator,' through the Microsoft form or an email. The Innovation team then posts the idea on the ideas portal, making it publicly accessible. The submission can be a fully formed concept or a rough idea that needs refinement. At this stage, accessibility is crucial—anyone at 12 Wing can contribute ideas, removing barriers to participation.

Evaluation—Once submitted, the Innovation Team assesses the idea. The Originator and the relevant senior leaders are notified if a preexisting solution exists or the idea falls outside the Wing's authority. If the idea demonstrates potential, the Innovation Team assigns a senior manager, referred to internally as a Facilitator, to assist the Originator in developing and refining the concept.

Development – The Originator and Facilitator work together to explore the idea's feasibility. This may involve research, stakeholder engagement, and resource assessment. During this phase, potential roadblocks are identified early to prevent future delays.

Presentation – When the pair is ready to present their idea, the facilitator arranges a meeting with an authorized person who can implement it, such as Approving Authority. The Originator then presents the idea to a decision-maker using a structured template, including the problem, solution, and expected benefits. Depending on the outcome, the idea might be approved for immediate implementation, need further refinement, or be escalated to another authority level (e.g., RCAF-wide initiatives).

Implementation—Once approved, the Originator takes ownership of executing the idea, following the direction provided in writing by the Approving Authority in the Briefing Outcome Form. The Innovation Team remains available for guidance and acts as a supportive Project Management Office or PMO, but the Originator and relevant operational teams drive implementation.

Feedback – Innovation does not stop at implementation. Continuous feedback loops ensure that ideas evolve and improve based on usage. Updates are communicated through the Innovation Portal, briefings, and direct emails so the Wing can track progress. This phase ensures that successful innovations are measured, refined, and scaled when applicable.

By structuring our innovation process, we eliminated confusion, enhanced transparency, and ensured every idea had a clear pathway from concept to execution. Ideas no longer disappeared into bureaucracy; instead, they transformed into actionable solutions that enhanced operations, morale, and efficiency at 12 Wing.

? Why Accessibility Matters

The hierarchical structure encompasses military organizations and often suppresses innovative ideas from lower ranks because senior leaders lack accessible pathways to receive such submissions. The process remains ambiguous, prompting some individuals to cease contributing their ideas as they perceive the system as challenging or time-consuming. We needed to put an end to this pattern of behaviour.

Our primary objective was to establish a seamless idea submission process to eliminate any potential reasons individuals might have for withholding their suggestions. We aimed to reduce access barriers to activate the existing unexpressed creative potential.

Leveraging Existing Resources

We examined our current resources because we decided against designing a brand-new system. We believed 12 Wing personnel would employ our process only if it corresponded seamlessly with their regular activities. A couple of essential resources were conveniently available to us.

◇ SharePoint

Base personnel frequently accessed SharePoint, which served as their leading communication portal, thus making it ideal as an innovation portal destination. Organizing our innovation portal as a central display on the splash page proved to be the right decision.

◇ Business Cards with QR Codes

Sometimes, simpler is better. Nick had the idea of creating innovation cards with our submission forms' QR codes. People could read the code through their smartphones to launch the form directly so they could provide their ideas quickly.

◇ Rotating Banner Ads

A basic banner advertisement appeared on the 12 Wing SharePoint homepage. Every user who logged on to the system automatically saw the prominent reminder that the innovation submission portal was accessible with a single click.

◇ Physical Posters

Even though digital tools work effectively, various users prefer physical notifications for communication. The squadron received big and small posters placed throughout every space. The posters included both the QR code and an overview of the procedure. Anyone accessing any area should find an accessible reminder that leads directly to the innovation portal.

Aside from digital methods, the direct approach remains essential in reaching out to others.

The user-friendly online form was insufficient, so we approached individuals in person. Direct interaction would produce the best results. People who encounter you in person will understand the straightforward nature of the submission process and correctly interpret your genuine desire for their ideas.

◇ Visiting Every Section

Nick and I established a personal objective to explore every area of the base at least once. The visits conveyed our commitment to innovation and process education, emphasizing any idea that posed value. Our physical presence allowed us to establish trust so people understood this initiative came from the bottom up.

◇ Q&A Sessions

Users generally refrain from expressing their questions when online interactions occur. During person-to-person engagement, they asked questions about their incomplete ideas and the evaluation process, making it clear they wanted direction. Our quick response reassured us because we insisted any sketchy notion would be considered.

💡 Lessons Learned

- 🔨 **Ease of Access is Key:** In streamlining idea-submission processes by removing complex steps, we gave users access to a simple submission form via a direct link/QR code and thus increased participation. The key takeaway? Customers value simple choices.

- 🔨 **Visibility Boosts Participation:** People unaware of our program won't use it. Our primary marketing approach featured posters, banner ads, and business cards— reminders about easy idea submission—with interest and excitement growing following staff idea implementation.

- 🔨 **In-Person Outreach Builds Trust:** Digital systems can't replace real conversations, our presence signaling our dedication/care and enabling feedback collection beyond email;

face-to-face interaction makes attendees feel respected and heard.

Making innovation accessible isn't just about having a system—it's also about ensuring that people can and want to use it. By simplifying processes, increasing visibility, and fostering trust through personal engagement, we have removed barriers to participation.

Now, let's explore how to create an accessible submission process that encourages idea-sharing and engagement within your organization.

🗣 Practical Advice

- ☑ **Start with the platform your organization already uses**—SharePoint or Slack. People are more likely to use tools that fit into their daily routines.
- ☑ **Keep it simple:** Limit submission steps to three. Streamline if necessary.
- ☑ **Promote Visibility:** Share your idea through emails, posters, banner ads, and briefings.

Daily activities should include innovation as an essential part

12 Wing needed our main effort to create innovations that fit their organizational culture. The team would get better at sharing ideas because a simple process would make these opportunities easy to access. What started as a joke about lost ideas became a real

process that provided new solutions for our organ-ization.

The key takeaway is that organizations gain from eliminating obstacles between people and innovative work. Any factor hindering employees from sharing ideas should be removed because fear and complexity can confuse them. Simplifying the process leads to better idea generation and increases the chances of finding transformative solutions for the workplace.

When innovation methods are easily accessible at all levels of the organization, all departments can contribute. A good idea submission process allows employees to cultivate their innovation potential at every level.

Your creative capture system will succeed if you follow these suggestions in its design. The process should be easy to access and straightforward since direct human interaction is important. You will be amazed by the many suggestions you receive when you implement this approach because of your effort.

The Facilitator Model: The Power of the Command Team

Colonel Holmes observed Major Veenhof and my collaboration during our meetings with him. Nick and I's working relationship reminded him of the importance of 'Command Team' officers and NCMs working collaboratively early in their careers to forge bonds that form the foundation of future leadership teams within the RCAF.

❓ Why Command Teams Matter

The success of military missions relies significantly on the working relationship between officers and non-commissioned members (NCMs) under most military conditions. Within command structures, officers handle strategic levels, while NCMs maintain technical expertise and operate from an operational standpoint. The strategic perspective of command personnel seamlessly integrates with the operational knowledge gained from field experience, creating an effective partnership.

Our innovation team had two purposes for Col Holmes. He viewed it as an operational blueprint for enhanced officer-NCM connections and utilized it to gather new ideas. The program was a cultural shaping initiative focused on developing the Royal Canadian Air Force (RCAF) into its future state.

Breaking Down Hierarchical Barriers

A facilitator structure in the 12 Wing Innovation Team automatically dissolved traditional military hierarchies while creating an equalized working environment. Here's how:

Collaborative Problem-Solving

The innovation projects between NCMs and officers thrived without rank-related barriers impacting their performance. All team members shared their ideas and contributions while conducting tests before developing improved solutions. Through direct collaboration, NCMs understood how leaders allocate resources, while office personnel gained insight into the significance of technical expertise.

Mutual Respect

Observing leaders generates more genuine respect than being ordered to respect someone due to their rank. This collaborative opportunity showcased to officers the valuable skills that NCMs could contribute while illustrating to NCMs the impact of leadership in making critical decisions. The mutual understanding fostered real admiration beyond simply adhering to basic rules.

Ongoing Communication

Standard hierarchical information flow leads to significant delays. Introducing facilitators who integrate officers and NCMs creates a two-way information system that accelerates idea exchange while facilitating direct feedback and concerns in both directions. Quick decision-making occurs in a workplace environment that values input from personnel at all levels.

Developing Future Leaders

Real life situations are more effective than classroom sessions for developing leadership skills. The Innovation Team's early career exposure to military personnel and police officers fostered the growth of essential leadership traits grounded in mutual respect.

Equal Opportunities to Contribute

Ranks did not affect participation in the Innovation Program. NCMs acquired valuable leadership experience by refining their presentation skills for proposal submissions and managing their innovation submission from start to finish.

Building Confidence

Encouraging organizational members to engage with the innovation team is important for building a strong foundation for the RCAF's growth.

Col Holmes recognized that the Air Force strengthens when command teams showcase their full potential at all levels. Collaborations between officers and NCMs enhance trust and communication, benefiting the RCAF for many years and even decades.

The collaborative spirit members develop at 12 Wing becomes a lasting part of their contributions during future assignments within the RCAF.

💡 Lessons Learned

- 🔨 **Collaboration is Crucial:** Strong officer-NCM partnerships grow via mutual, relationship-building support. Facing challenges together creates lasting trust.
- 🔨 **Innovation as a Leadership Tool:** Effective leadership development goes beyond the result; it involves the entire journey to achieve that result. Innovation requires skills in planning, execution, adaptation, and

teamwork, helping to build leadership qualities and team coordination.

- 🪓 **Culture** is built every day through daily actions, interactions, and shared experiences, fostering collective success across military ranks.

🗣️ Practical Advice

- ☑ Create Mixed Teams consisting of junior and senior members. Form workgroups with Officers and NCM members when possible, allowing enthusiastic members to share their perspectives.
- ☑ Focus on Real Challenges and prioritize practical tasks over theoretical ones to develop respect and skills through real-world solutions.
- ☑ Encourage Open Dialogue; leaders should ask questions rather than give orders. Valuing staff input helps break down hierarchies.
- ☑ Stay Flexible and rapidly adapt to operational failures by changing team dynamics and roles for innovative ideas.

⭐ Remember

Building a strong command team takes time because teamwork and trust come from solving problems and learning from each other. Good strategic thinking and technical skills create a setting where relationships can grow through innovative work. Your current financial investment in collaboration between units will lead to a more connected organization that achieves better results in the future.

Col. Holmes was absolutely right when he remarked that early bond formation between officers and NCMs has lasting consequences that influence their entire military careers and the organizations they serve. This approach, which spans from the 12 Wing to the Royal Canadian Air Force, starts with fostering enduring success.

Preparing the Pitch: Turning Ideas into Actionable Proposals

Human beings often find it challenging to develop presentations from excellent concepts, even when those ideas are exceptionally brilliant. Such remarkable concepts seldom reach implementation despite lacking intrinsic flaws because their originators do not grasp how to craft compelling pitches. The 12 Wing Innovation Team aims to transform basic ideas into executable proposals.

The Gap Between Inspiration and Execution

The ability to be inspired is distinct from the process of putting that inspiration into action. The 12 Wing staff observed many brilliant concepts among personnel but found a limited capacity among employees to execute their plans. Questions like "What should I do next?" and "How will I demonstrate my idea's value?" continually confused the idea originators.

We established a supportive process grounded in project management to guide individuals through their idea development journey. Our team goes beyond mere facilitation; we actively assist idea developers in refining their concepts, gaining vali- dation for their ideas, and honing their presentation skills.

Organizing the Pitch Demands More Than Simple Presentation Slides

People often perceive pitches as slide-based presentations featuring functional visual elements, even though content is just as crucial for making a strong case. The organization provides presentation frameworks for individuals to develop engaging visuals and clear business presentations. The process encompasses more than merely crafting an appealing slide design.

◇ Focus on the Real Problem

Our process guides originators in identifying the challenges their startup concept genuinely needs to tackle. Many organizations employ root cause analysis in this process. People often devise solutions for symptoms but overlook the fundamental issues, leading to recurring instances of the same problem.

◇ Tell a Story With Data

The leaders in your organization value statistical data because it shows how your concept applies to existing operational situations. We advise originators to collect relevant metrics through time reduction measures, cost savings, and user satisfaction levels before presenting them in an easy-to-understand format.

◇ Align With Operational Needs

A successful pitch requires connecting the idea to the essential objectives of 12 Wing operations. Demonstrating how your idea supports the broader organizational goals will enhance its persuasive impact on decision-makers regarding efficiency improvement, morale-boosting, and mission readiness.

▢ Coaching and Feedback

Our fundamental role involves delivering coaching services by assisting personnel with their delivery practice, helping them develop their statements, and teaching them how to prepare for questions. We evaluate the proposal's organization and information collection while validating its connection to operational needs. The support we provide distinguishes between fading worthwhile concepts and achieving success approval.

◇ Guided Rehearsals

Our team regularly conducts trial presentations that allow originators to evaluate their pitches without facing real decision-makers. This practice enables originators to grasp the flow of their presentations to identify their most vulnerable points.

◇ Root Cause Analysis Workshops

We facilitate concise workshops for individuals seeking further assistance in identifying essential aspects of their challenges. Participants leave the workshops with an enhanced understanding of what contributes to their issues, strengthening their proposed solutions' effectiveness.

◇ Continuous Support

The team continues to support the project after the pitch phase by helping to categorize solutions based on the feedback received. We also assist the proposal originator in revising their submission due to concerns raised by decision-makers.

❓ Why This Matters

Submitting high-quality, data-rich proposals to a leader's desk leads to remarkable chances of acceptance. Simply stating that a proposed solution could alleviate the problem is insufficient; researchers must demonstrate its benefits and necessity. The proposal needs to explain its positive impact, provide support for fundamental needs, and include a visual presentation of future outcomes. The coaching process helps creators pass crucial assessments, ensuring their potentially stellar ideas remain visible throughout proposed changes.

◇ Boosting Innovation Culture

Successful idea implementation generates a motivational effect that encourages more people to share their concepts with the organization. Due to this demonstrated success, the process showcases its effectiveness as individuals choose to present their proposals.

◇ **Building Confidence:**

A successful pitch run fosters participants' essential skills in critical thinking, presentation, and stakeholder relationship management. The confidence gained empowers employees to take initiative in their work environment, resulting in a team of self-directed professionals.

◇ **Aligning With Organizational Goals:**

The final assessment of any proposed idea should focus on improving the 12 Wing's operational capabilities, morale, and unit readiness. Our structured system ensures that every pitch delivers value beyond being an interesting but ultimately unimpactful "cool idea."

♀ **Lessons Learned**

- 🔨 A clear pitch boosts success. Slides lacking clarity and evidence lose decision-makers attention. A strong presentation with solid evidence increases your chances of approval.
- 🔨 Root cause analysis is essential**; addressing** symptoms rarely fixes the core problem. Focusing on major root causes in proposals strengthens requests from originators.

Bottomup BREAKTHROUGH

When teams struggle to share their ideas effectively, valuable concepts can fail to gain traction. To help overcome this, we offer practical advice for your pitch, providing tools and mentorship to empower your project advocacy.

🗣 Practical Advice

- ☑ **Know Your Audience:** Customize your presentation to align with your audience's main business objectives and explain how your idea solves a key issue.
- ☑ **Use Data:** Include statistics and examples to strengthen your points and boost credibility.
- ☑ **Simplify Your Presentation:** Use minimal text and clear visuals to stay focused and guide your audience through the key points.
- ☑ **Practice:** Rehearse your presentation and refine it based on feedback.

Moving From Idea to Execution

The 12 Wing Innovation Team requires more than just collecting ideas; its primary purpose is to transform concepts into concrete improvements. A combination of structured coaching methods directs inspirational ideas toward full execution, ensuring that the best concepts can become successful.

Turning your inspiration into action consists of refining your thoughts, gathering information, and creating a presentation format that clearly explains the problem. The right preparation and expert guidance transform simple ideas into executable proposals that lead to meaningful change.

The Approval Process: How Ideas Get the Green Light

Human beings fail to turn their brilliant concepts into presentations despite their original quality. Brilliant ideas fail to become operational despite being faultless because originators do not know how to create persuasive pitches that advance their concepts. The 12 Wing Innovation Team uses basic concepts to develop executable proposals.

Implementation and Feedback: Continuous Improvement and Feedback Loops

Congratulations on getting approval for your idea! But guess what? The innovative process begins after you receive approval rather than ending at that point. The approval of an innovation represents only the first phase of work. Implementing an innovation sets the stage, but demonstrating its ongoing success through regular improvement yields genuine results. The true achievement at 12 Wing occurs when innovative ideas thrive over time instead of being launched success-fully.

The Importance of Tracking and Accountability

Managing multiple ideas at once can result in several concepts being lost. Our key team member, Nick, developed the SharePoint Idea Tracker document and established an Innovation library on SharePoint to store it and support our project development activities. All our ideas can be found on this digital platform, which serves as a project-tracking center. The system received each proposal containing information about the idea creator, the facilitator who managed the initiative, and key deadline targets.

- The idea tracker provides a solution for anyone who wants to know the status of the maintenance app proposal because it transparently shows 'approved,' 'in progress,' and 'completed.'
- Regular updates on the tracker allowed us to identify execution challenges at the beginning of their development. The system enabled facilitators to request additional resources simultaneously while informing originators about their need for new input.
- One or multiple facilitators carried forward each idea's development. Everyone understood their specific tasks because each person had a straightforward assignment.

Why Bi-Weekly Follow-Ups?

Our system operated independently of relying solely on the Idea Tracker. Both facilitators and originators engaged in check-in meetings with our team twice a month. These checkpoints served as assessment points for your initiatives.

- Frequent team check-ins reduce the risk of work projects stalling, as team members can lose focus on their assignments. The brief discussions held bi-weekly kept project ideas fresh in everyone's mind.
- The project requires early intervention to secure software access and a budget for new tools. Our bi-monthly meetings enabled us to identify potential issues early, allowing for quick resolutions before they developed into larger problems.
- Originators possess valuable insights, and the facilitators still need support for their initiatives. Regular team meetings furnished facilitators with essential support and resource backup to advance their initiatives.

Feedback Loops: Evolving the Idea

Implementing in the real world provides value by revealing what works effectively and what does not. Due to its significance, this process necessitates essential feedback systems. We collected project data and user feedback, noting any unexpected issues immediately after launching each initiative. Develo-

pers utilized this data to adjust their project development strategies.

- We actively implemented the Minimum Viable
  Product (MVP) philosophy in our operations.
  First, we launched a foundational version, which
  we then upgraded based on user feedback.
- The planning process will always face unexpected challenges since user feedback remains unpredictable. Testing the final product
  through regular personal use allows us to
  uncover hidden issues.
- Our initial results could function, but user
  evaluations revealed opportunities to refine
  operations, enhance functionalities, or change
  direction entirely.

💡 Lessons Learned

Tracking Ideas to Prevent Stagnation

- The Idea Tracker centralizes information,
  eliminating the need to search through emails
  or lost conversations. It promotes accountability
  by keeping everyone informed about ongoing
  activities.
- Regular Check-Ins Keep Progress on Track.
  Ideas can fade without consistent monitoring. A
  regular follow-up system helps maintain
  project direction and quickly addresses issues.
- Feedback Loops Drive Innovation Implementing an idea is just the start. Success comes from

ongoing improvements based on **lived** experiences, showcasing the power of the MVP mindset.

Capturing ideas is just the beginning—what happens next determines their success. Regular check-ins, clear accountability, and feedback loops ensure that ideas don't stagnate but evolve into impactful solutions. Now, let's explore practical advice for continuous improvement, which will help you refine and enhance ideas over time.

👤 Practical Advice

- ☑ **Centralized Tracking System:** A simple spreadsheet shared via a common tool can solve many issues. Ensure all teammates can easily access and edit the system.
- ☑ **Schedule Regular Check-Ins:** Your team should establish regular check-ins and then decide on an appropriate meeting schedule, whether
- ☑ **Encourage Honest Feedback:** People often hesitate to share issues and challenges.

Sustaining Innovation Through CI

Implementing change takes time, and celebrating milestones keeps teams motivated. At 12 Wing, continuous improvement became a part of the culture, with staff actively refining ideas and contributing enhancements. Leaders who valued feedback fostered innovation. True innovation is ongoing, relying on user feedback and adapting to needs, ensuring ideas remain relevant and successful.

To sustain momentum:

- Foster **accountability** by planning for the future development of approved ideas.
- Encourage **ownership** by reinforcing the value of every contribution.
- Support **long-term innovation** by embedding continuous improvement into daily operations.

Organizations can transform great ideas into lasting, impactful solutions by maintaining focus beyond the initial approval stage.

Sustaining innovation requires not only the right mindset but also the right tools. The next chapter explores simple, practical tools that help organizations streamline their innovation process, gather feedback effectively, and turn ideas into action.

CHAPTER 6

SIMPLE TOOLS FOR DRIVING INNOVATION

*"Tools are just tools. They don't have any power.
Not unless you give it to them."*

MAGGIE STIEFVATER

Why do some organizations rapidly develop and implement new ideas while others grapple with persistent roadblocks and resistance? The key difference lies in creativity and the existence of a structured framework that directs ideas from conception to execution. This chapter delves into how organizations—corporations, nonprofits, or mission-driven teams—can establish a scalable innovation process that prevents ideas from getting lost in bureaucracy. We will outline a step-by-step approach to capturing ideas, refining them into compelling pitches, securing approvals, and ultimately transforming them into tangible improvements.

By the end of this chapter, you'll have a practical blueprint for establishing an innovation pipeline within your organization that generates fresh ideas and ensures they lead to real, measurable impact.

Leveraging Microsoft Forms for Idea Collection

Do you possess a brilliant concept that seems too time-intensive to present to your work team? The staff at 12 Wing frequently experienced this obstacle, leading us to create a platform that simplifies idea-sharing procedures. The most potent fundamental tool we adopted was Microsoft Forms. This explanation will make using Microsoft Forms as an innovation tool apparent and guide you toward using the same approach for your business needs.

Why Microsoft Forms?

When Nick and I discussed gathering ideas during our initial conversation, we discovered complexity as a primary obstacle. The structure of idea submission, when complex with paperwork and multiple steps, would cause people to avoid participation. The system needed quick access on any device through a user-friendly interface. The user-friendly interface of Microsoft Forms proved to be a perfect fit because it addressed all required needs.

◇ Ease of use

The form setup process requires no specialized technical expertise or dedicated IT personnel for creating or managing purposes.

◇ Ease of access

Every person can access forms on different devices, including mobile phones and computers, through tablets, regardless of location.

◇ Convenient notifications

The system provides right-away notifications that inform facilitators whenever someone submits their idea, even though the process can continue running in the background. The system supports continuing forward progress and enables immediate follow-up activities.

How We Made It Work

Microsoft Forms operation at 12 Wing followed these exact steps:

Step 1: Creating the Form

We kept it straightforward. Just a few short questions:

- What's your idea?
- Why is this important?
- How could we implement it?
- Who should we follow up with?

The short nature of the questions helped eliminate any fears about completing the form process.

Step 2. The system utilizes QR Codes to enable fast access to the form in

Multiple forms of our business cards, informational posters, printed QR codes, and flyers were distributed throughout our base. People with ideas could easily access the form through QR code scanning before completing the submission within a few seconds.

Step 3: Promoting Everywhere

Visibility was key. We integrated those QR codes with links at three points on our SharePoint homepage, email signatures, and meeting rooms. Our design for easy accessibility led to increased submission flow from our users.

Real-World Example: Multiple Communication Channels

When we distributed these forms through multiple sharing channels, we received numerically higher levels of idea submissions. We obtained over 100 ideas for the entire Wing from the first few months of operation. Each submitted idea provided essential information, allowing immediate solutions to genuine company problems.

✂ Practical Tip

To implement Microsoft Forms for innovation enhancement, you should follow these usage guidelines:

- The form must be brief and uncomplicated because additional questions or complexity will deter users from finishing it. Users abandon surveys that require longer than three minutes of their time.
- Microsoft Forms should accommodate mobile devices because most users prefer smartphone use over computer access.
- Regular form promotion happens through email alerts, phone-friendly links, and meeting presentations to maintain visibility.

💡 Lessons Learned

- Simplified idea submission processes increased the number of participants.
- Easy access through any device enabled people to submit ideas when inspiration hit.
- A fast notification system built trust because our team could respond rapidly to demonstrate the value of submitted concepts to contributors.

The Bottom Line

Innovation requires neither sophisticated nor expensive equipment to succeed. Microsoft Forms served as our tool for straightforward idea collection while eliminating every obstacle that prevented users from participating. Consider making this trial because one straightforward form could lead to your team's central innovation.

SharePoint as an Innovation Hub: Organizing and Tracking Progress

The workplace has often created situations where excellent work ideas get lost due to post-it note forgettable lapses or clouded in disorganized email systems. We decided to prevent such situations from occurring at 12 Wing. A basic ordered system became essential since it would handle all ideas while showing their advancement stages and maintaining team awareness. SharePoint proved lucky for us since we transformed it into our innovation hub.

Why We Chose SharePoint

Our Innovation Team received many submissions, which forced Nick and me to understand that a spreadsheet was insufficient. The organization needed a streamlined, centralized platform for all ideas to gain complete visibility. Nick entrusted me with Deputy Innovation Officer duties, enabling me to construct our Idea Portal on SharePoint. Why SharePoint?

◇ Already Familiar

All personnel within the 12 Wing depended on SharePoint for daily operations. Developing the existing system proved more beneficial than creating an entirely new one.

◇ No Extra Cost or Setup

Using SharePoint required no fancy software nor outside help because our existing system was sufficient to manage the process. SharePoint was ready to go.

◇ Flexible and Customizable:

Users could customize the toolset in SharePoint to match our requirements without programming intricacies.

How We Set It Up

1. Leveraging SharePoint as an Ideas Portal

Nick and I created the Idea Portal using SharePoint to transform scattered ideas into organized projects with a structured workflow. Each idea had a dedicated SharePoint page outlining key details such as the originator (the idea submitter), the facilitator (the person driving the idea forward), and the approving authority (responsible for final decisions). This system ensured clarity in roles, streamlined decision-making, and made daily innovation actionable and trackable

2. Automatic Submission & Tracking

Ideas were collected through Microsoft Forms submissions. After a submission is made, I will receive an automated email notification. After reviewing the idea, Nick or I would list it in our Idea tracker.

This was done using an Excel sheet to provide a quick overview of all submitted ideas. This process allowed us to quickly access the Excel sheet for quick reference while maintaining detailed tracking of our SharePoint pages.

3. Real-Time Status Updates

Each idea page included three essential elements for tracking purposes: the original submission material was accessible, so readers did not have to sift through the email to discover the presented concept.

The short notes provided status information on each idea's progress, including its status of being under review, approved, implemented, and completed. Ongoing posts prevented misunderstandings between team members. The page system enabled anyone to view an idea's exact status through straightforward page access.

🔑 Key Takeaways

- 🔒 **Keep It Simple:** We created a simple system with only the necessary features. The idea pages focused on essentials, avoiding un-necessary details. This simplicity made the system user-friendly.
- 🔒 **Promote the Portal:** A SharePoint page doesn't help if no one knows it exists. Team members

were encouraged to share ideas and updates through the portal.

🔒 **Regular Check-Ins:** Effective check-ins require follow-up. Facilitators met regularly to discuss issues, track progress, and set priorities, ensuring ideas continued growing.

💡 Lessons Learned

📌 Centralized Idea Management is crucial. It prevents valuable ideas from being lost by keeping them in one place, ensuring they are reviewed and considered for implementation.

📌 Transparency fosters trust and engagement. Access to real-time updates on ideas motivates people to participate and contribute.

📌 Assigning facilitators fosters culture change and leadership development. They lead innovation, guide their teams, and promote continuous improvement across the 12 Wing.

Completing the Vision

Nick and I envisioned the 12 Wing Innovation Team as a network that fosters innovation among all members. Anyone wishing to achieve similar results within their organization should begin with fundamental concepts. Your organization should utilize an existing platform, such as SharePoint or Google Sites, to create its Idea Portal, as all platforms can support the concept.

Business Cards with QR Codes: Making Participation Easy

We knew that a complicated submission process would discourage participation from the start. To make idea sharing quick and effortless, we integrated QR codes into business cards, providing instant access to the submission form.

The Challenge: Lowering Barriers to Participation

People are busy. If submitting an idea requires too many steps, they'll delay—or abandon—the process entirely. We needed a frictionless solution that allowed anyone to participate within seconds.

The Solution: One-Step Access

By printing QR codes on business cards, we created a simple, direct way to submit ideas:

- A smartphone can scan the provided QR code.
- Instantly access the submission form.
- A member can submit their concept within sixty seconds using the available tool.

This approach **removed friction**, increased engagement, and made innovation accessible to everyone.

❓ Why It Worked

The main benefit of business cards with QR codes is their ease of use. Staff can quickly access QR codes in meetings and break rooms to submit ideas anytime. The QR codes provide a simple way to fill out the submission form.

Additionally, the cards remove excuses. By offering them, we ensured that the minimal time needed for submissions was a direct reply to anyone who said they had no time.

How We Distributed Them

We organized the distribution approach methodically.

We delivered cards to all participants during each program's introduction to new groups.

Our team motivated supervisors to keep a stack of cards in their workplaces so they could distribute them to their team members.

The squadron offices, meeting rooms, and busy public areas received cards as strategic placements.

Unexpected Benefits

- Continuous exposure to the innovation program happened through visual reminder cards.
- Viewers of individuals scanning QR codes often started discussing their ideas for submission.

- Leadership Engagement improved through tangible tools because they could distribute these tools to their teams for participation stimulation.

💡 Lessons Learned

- 🔨 People use systems that offer straightforward interfaces since simplicity enhances user engagement.
- 🔨 Action-based performance increases significantly when physical tools such as business cards replace electronic communications like emails.
- 🔨 Speedy submission procedures between idea conception and submission maintain high participation rates.

We find the best solutions through simple methods rather than complex ones. Business cards with QR codes are practical tools that make it easy to participate in innovation. This approach ensures valuable ideas are not lost, as submitting them used to be difficult for the team.

CHAPTER 7

LEADERSHIP STYLES THAT DRIVE INNOVATION & MENTORSHIP

"Innovation distinguishes between a leader and a follower."

STEVE JOBS

Leadership involves more than just giving orders; it requires inspiring individuals to generate new ideas and build their confidence as active contributors to innovation. The leadership behaviour at 12 Wing is crucial in determining whether the organization nurtures or undermines a culture of creative innovation.

This section covers leadership styles that promote innovation, specifically transformational, steward, and servant leadership. It explains that transformational leaders create visionary goals, steward leaders efficiently manage resources, and servant leaders enhance team capabilities. The importance of mentorship in developing leaders and fostering an innovative culture is also discussed.

After this lesson, readers will understand how choosing the right leaders energizes teams and nurtures creativity, as well as the essential skills for innovative leadership and the role of mentorship.

What is Transformational Leadership?

Transformational leaders drive motivation by helping individuals achieve significant objectives beyond personal tasks. They inspire their teams to share innovative ideas, take calculated risks, and seek continuous improvement. These leaders accomplish their objectives by consistently enhancing the performance of everyone who works with them. At 12 Wing, transformational leadership principles are demonstrated by leaders who embody these traits.

We have witnessed true examples of transformational leadership under the guidance of LCol Baldasaro, Col Holmes, LCol Lawrence, and CWO Wezenbeek. Their commands inspired critical thinking and innovation and fostered an environment where creativity thrived and challenges were met with collaborative solutions. Without the contributions of these leaders, establishing the 12 Wing Innovation Team would not have been possible.

Bottomup BREAKTHROUGH

In the subsequent sections, I will detail the essential leadership traits that have made this culture of innovation not just theoretical but practical and replicable within any organization.

Characteristics

◇ Set clear and inspiring goals.

These leaders showed what the tasks meant to accomplish instead of merely expressing tasks alone.

◇ Encouraged creative thinking.

They obtained suggestions from their team members and actively engaged in dialogue, which made employees believe their comments added value.

◇ Empowered others to act.

Transformational leaders empower team members to initiate new projects and make independent decisions. This style fosters innovation, significantly contributing to 12 Wing's success in multiple ways.

◇ Empowered Teams, Meaningful Impact

Transformational leaders engage workers to show their appreciation, foster motivation, and boost morale toward contribution.

🗣 Practical Advice

☑ Foster a Growth Mindset and encourage continuous learning, adaptability, and innovation by empowering employees to take initiative and experiment with new ideas.

☑ Lead with Vision and Purpose, clearly communicating the bigger picture and aligning team efforts with organizational goals to create meaning and motivation.

☑ Cultivate Trust and Autonomy, allowing teams to make decisions while providing guidance and support, fostering accountability and ownership.

What is Steward Leadership?

Steward leadership is a leadership style that emphasizes a long-term, holistic approach to guiding organizations and their employees. Unlike operational managers who prioritize efficiency and immediate task execution, steward leaders focus on sustainable growth, ethical practices, and the well-being of both their teams and stakeholders. They create an environment that fosters individual development, encouraging team members to thrive, contribute significantly, and recognize their roles within a larger mission.

At 12 Wing, steward leadership was demonstrated through leaders encouraging innovation and empowering people. These leaders acted as custodians of the organization's purpose and its employees, ensuring each action was aligned with the organization's overarching goals and the welfare of individuals within it.

Characteristics of Steward Leadership

◇ Set clear and meaningful goals.

Steward leaders went beyond simply defining tasks—they ensured that every mission had a deeper purpose, connecting individual efforts to the long-term success of the organization and the well-being of those involved.

◇ Encouraged shared ownership of ideas.

Rather than imposing solutions, they listened, facilitated collaboration, and empowered individuals to contribute their insights. By nurturing a culture of open dialogue, they ensured that team members felt valued and responsible for the organization's future.

◇ Promoted ethical decision-making and long-term sustainability.

Instead of chasing short-term wins, steward leaders prioritized solutions that created lasting positive impacts—on people, the mission, and the broader community. Their leadership was grounded in service, not self-interest.

🗣 Practical Advice

☑ Actively engage with others by listening attentively. Doing so fosters an environment where team members feel encouraged to take initiative and present their ideas.

☑ Recognize and celebrate your team's accomplishments and innovative suggestions. Highlighting small successes can enhance morale and inspire creative thinking, leading to continuous achievement.

☑ Model the behaviours and attitudes you expect from your team. Your commitment to innovation will inspire team members to embrace and drive change towards innovative outcomes.

What is Servant Leadership?

To me, true leadership isn't about power; it's about service. When I went to Plan Qulliq and later proposed the Innovation Team at 12 Wing, my goal wasn't personal advancement or recognition. It was about removing obstacles for my peers, even if it meant working extra hours and shouldering additional responsibilities. I saw how talented bureaucratic roadblocks and outdated processes held back individuals. I knew that innovation couldn't thrive in an environment where great ideas stalled before they could grow.

Servant leadership is rooted in the belief that leaders exist to empower others, not to command them. I didn't want people at 12 Wing to feel like they had to struggle just to be heard—I wanted to build a system that supported them, amplified their ideas, and made it easier for them to contribute to meaningful change. That's why I proposed the Innovation Team. It wasn't about creating something new for the sake of innovation—it was about ensuring that the people around me had a clear, accessible path to make an impact.

Characteristics

◇ Adaptive Leadership in Action

Leaders adjusted their leadership approach on the fly to shift between directive involvement and providing autonomous freedom to team members.

◇ Personalized Leadership for Maximum Impact

These leaders exhibited the ability to identify each team member's attributes and limitations because they structured their approach according to individual characteristics.

◇ Situational Awareness Fuels Leadership

They maintained a precise view of situations to choose appropriate leadership styles for every difficulty.

🗣 Practical Advice

- ☑ Carefully note how your team members act when facing diverse conditions. You need to determine the right moments to provide instructions, offer support when needed, and give authority to control situations.
- ☑ Clearly explain your leadership approaches to every team member through clear communication, thus earning their trust in your choices.

☑ Reserve your commitment to a single appro-ach. Leaders must be adaptive by changing their management style to address various innovation needs that emerge within their team.

💡 Lessons Learned

🔨 Leaders who generate the most effective results customize their methods according to what benefits their teams and the present circumstances require.

🔨 A flexible approach to meeting team require-ments creates protected conditions for enhanced innovation to develop.

🔨 Team member knowledge enables leaders to modify leadership techniques according to their team member's specific skills and experiences.

The Importance of Mentorship in Innovation Programs

Have you ever had someone professionally who helped guide you through new ideas? Those who have experienced mentorship understand its immense value for a team's success. At 12 Wing Shearwater, mentorship was crucial in driving our innovation program forward. In the following section, we will explore the importance of mentorship in organi-zations and how to implement it effectively.

What Exactly is Mentorship?

The foundation of mentorship consists of two people joining forces when one possesses more excellent professional prowess (the mentor role), and one requires guidance (the mentee role). The innovative aspect requires mentorship to extend beyond conventional boundaries. Developing innovation skills requires more than transferring information since it allows people to exhibit confident and creative innovation alongside effective execution.

At 12 Wing, effective mentors

- Mentors offer open discussions about their successful and unsuccessful experiences, guiding mentees in preventing mistakes and making superior choices.
- They provided constant support and encouragement, allowing mentees to develop the confidence necessary to implement new, innovative processes.
- Mentors offer accurate, beneficial feedback to their mentees, leading them toward better developing their innovative concepts.

How Mentorship Drives Innovation

The impact of mentorship stands as a key factor in creating entrepreneurship. Here's what we found:

- Partnership with a mentor allows the mentee to acquire knowledge rapidly through practical case studies and recommendations. The mentorship process moves innovation forward by enabling mentees to avoid standard obstacles so they can dedicate their efforts to essential areas.

- Mentees become more willing to take strategic risks because they have a supporter who stands behind them. Correct innovation requires the unrestricted ability to test experimental concepts.
- A mentorship program helps teams bond better by strengthening trust, increasing respect, and fostering teamwork, which leads to active innovation.

💡 Lessons Learned

- 📌 Understanding that skilled mentors support them often leads mentees to act more confidently during their innovative projects.
- 📌 Knowledge sharing through mentorship enables mentees to avoid waste, speeding up their development process while conserving valuable resources and time.
- 📌 Long-Term Support Weighted toward Mentorship Activity Is Vital for Sustained Improvement of Innovation Processes from Start to Finish.
- 📌 Mentorship isn't just about guidance—it's a catalyst for confidence, efficiency, and long-term success in innovation. Mentors empower teams to navigate challenges and accelerate

progress by fostering knowledge sharing and providing sustained support.

Now, let's explore practical advice for effective mentorship, ensuring mentors and mentees maximize their impact and drive meaningful innovation.

🗣 Practical Advice

- ☑ Setting clear expectations helps mentors and mentees understand their roles and tasks. Regular check-ins build trust, making tracking progress, solving problems, and giving feedback easier. Creating a supportive space where mentees can freely share ideas is essential for success.
- ☑ At 12 Wing, mentorship speeds learning, builds confidence, and sparks creativity—important factors for meaningful change. When applied to innovation projects, mentorship helps teams reach their full potential and fosters a thriving culture of progress.

Innovation isn't without obstacles. The next chapter explores common barriers and how to navigate them to keep progress moving forward.

CHAPTER 8

OVERCOMING CHALLENGES AND BARRIERS TO INNOVATION

"The greatest barrier to success is the fear of failure."

SVEN GORAN ERIKSSON

Innovation isn't just about coming up with new ideas—it's about navigating resistance, skepticism, and structural barriers to turn those ideas into reality. No matter how passionate a team is or how valuable an idea may be, obstacles will always arise. The ability to identify and overcome these barriers is what separates successful innovation programs from those that never gain traction.

This chapter explores organizations' most common challenges when implementing innovation and provides practical strategies to address them. By understanding how to gain trust, handle feedback, learn from setbacks, and secure leadership support, you can drive meaningful change within your team or organization.

The Struggle for Legitimacy: Gaining Trust in a Structured System

Introducing change in a structured environment often meets resistance. People have set ways of working and usually distrust new initiatives, especially if previous attempts have failed. When we started our innovation program, there was skepticism at all levels. Some doubted its longevity, while others believed it would be another short-lived effort.

Instead of just explaining, we showed results. We started small, delivering clear improvements from which people could see and benefit directly.

How We Addressed Skepticism

Start Small, Prove Early – We identified quick wins that showed immediate value. Instead of large projects, we made small, impactful changes to simplify daily tasks. These successes built credibility.

Engage Skeptics as Allies – We welcomed critics into the process. Involving doubters helped convert some of our biggest skeptics into committed supporters.

Celebrate Success – Recognizing team contributions increased engagement. As real change happened, participation grew, fostering a culture that embraced innovation.

💡 Lessons Learned

- Trust is built through action, not words. The best way to overcome skepticism is by delivering results.
- Early wins create momentum. Start with projects that can be quickly implemented to prove the value of innovation.
- Inclusion transforms resistance into support. When people feel heard and involved, they are likelier to become advocates rather than critics.

Building trust and momentum is just the first step. To foster innovation, leaders need to encourage feedback. Constructive criticism helps improve ideas and ensures success. Next, we'll discuss how to manage feedback effectively—turning criticism into opportunities and resistance into teamwork.

Handling Feedback

Every new idea will face pushback. Concerns come from uncertainty, past failures, or fear of change, so resistance is normal. However, objections can be used as a chance to improve and develop ideas further.

Common Objections and How to Address Them

"We've always done it this way."

Resistance to change often comes from habit. Instead of dismissing concerns, we demonstrated how small process improvements could lead to significant time savings and efficiency gains.

"It won't work here."

Many doubters assume that new ideas work elsewhere but not in their specific environment. We countered this by piloting projects on a small scale, collecting data, and proving feasibility before full implementation.

"We've tried this before, and it failed."

Past failures don't mean an idea is bad—they mean there was something to learn. We analyzed previous attempts, identified what went wrong, and adjusted our approach accordingly.

🔑 **Key Takeaways**

- 🔒 Listen before responding. Instead of immediately defending an idea, take the time to understand concerns and acknowledge valid points.
- 🔒 Use data and current examples. Demonstrating success elsewhere can help build confidence in new initiatives.
- 🔒 Past failures are learning opportunities. You can refine an idea by analyzing what went wrong for a greater chance of success.

Turning Setbacks into Stepping Stones: Learning and Growing from Failure

Innovation isn't always easy—setbacks will occur. It is important to learn from them rather than allow them to stop progress. At 12 Wing, some of our early projects didn't go as expected. Instead of seeing them as failures, we saw them as learning opportunities.

How We Used Failure to Improve

- **Identify the Root Cause** – Instead of assuming an idea was flawed, we used root cause analysis to determine whether the issue was in execution, communication, or buy-in.
- **Adjust, Don't Abandon** – Many ideas needed tweaking, not discarding. By iterating on our approaches, we turned initial failures into eventual successes.
- **Normalize Experimentation**—We created an environment where taking calculated risks was encouraged, so team members weren't afraid to propose new ideas.

💡 Lessons Learned

🏷 Failure isn't the opposite of success—it's a step toward it. Treat setbacks as learning moments rather than roadblocks.

- Adjust, don't quit. If something doesn't work, refine and try again rather than abandoning it entirely.
- Encourage experimentation. A culture that embraces trial and error fosters long-term innovation.

Innovation requires resilience, but moving ahead without balance leads to burnout. Teams need to manage their energy alongside their ideas to ensure lasting progress. Preventing burnout creates an engaging and sustainable environment for improvement. Let's discuss how to keep momentum while ensuring well-being.

Preventing Burnout: Sustaining Innovation Over Time

Driving change is exciting, but it can also be exhausting. Even the best innovation efforts can lead to burnout without the right balance. We learned that sustaining momentum required intentional efforts to manage workloads, recognize achievements, and encourage breaks.

Strategies for Preventing Burnout

1. **Balance Workloads –** Innovation shouldn't be an extra burden. We ensured responsibilities were distributed evenly so no single person carried the full weight of implementation.

2. **Celebrate Regularly** – Recognition keeps morale high. We kept the team motivated and engaged by celebrating small and big wins.
3. **Encourage Downtime** – Rest fuels creativity. We built breaks to allow people to recharge, ultimately leading to better long-term results.

💡 Lessons Learned

- Pacing is essential. Innovation is a marathon, not a sprint—balance is necessary to sustain progress.
- Recognition fuels motivation. Taking time to acknowledge contributions keeps people engaged.
- Rest is part of the process. Overworked teams lose creativity and effectiveness; regular down-time leads to better results.

Sustaining innovation requires leadership that removes obstacles and supports teams. Let's see how leaders can drive change.

The Role of Senior Leadership in Breaking Barriers

Senior leaders maintain a fundamental responsibility to shape organizational culture and eliminate innovative obstacles in addition to their role in managerial decision-making. The leadership at 12 Wing Shearwater positively influenced innovation by actively backing these efforts. We will examine what enabled them to break barriers, the importance these breakthroughs had for the organization, and practical steps you can take to motivate such leadership within your team or organization.

Why Senior Leadership Matters

Senior leaders set the tone. An innovation program's performance depends heavily on its conduct and perspectives. 12 Wing demonstrated that supportive senior leaders vanquish obstacles while eliminating barriers preventing ideas from progressing from the concept phase to execution.

Strong senior leadership creates essential outcomes for the following reasons:

- Senior leaders possess the capability to eliminate barriers, including lengthy approval periods, bureaucratic impediments, and obstacles to transformation that threaten to halt innovation progress.
- Through leadership, teams can acquire resources and tools that enable their personnel to develop and execute new ideas.
- Such leaders develop trust by actively supporting innovation and showing employees their innovative ideas are valuable and embraced.

3 Ways Senior Leaders Supported Innovation at 12 Wing

Our senior leadership created ways to help us overcome obstacles through these actions:

Bottomup BREAKTHROUGH

1. Advocating for Change

The innovation program received public backing from our leaders, who actively promoted great ideas across the entire Wing through ongoing public praise. The initiative gained power because leaders publicly demonstrated their strong support of innovation, inspiring team members to participate.

2. Facilitating Quick Approvals

The approval process received simplified treatment by senior leadership to operate more efficiently. Decisions moved forward swiftly because the leaders ensured prompt conclusion of evaluations, allowing innovative ideas to transition right from pitch meetings into execution.

3. Encouraging Open Communication

The leadership team maintained a policy of active dialogue, which made every member of the organizational chart feel secure about sharing their thoughts, including personnel at lower ranks. Our open environment made colleagues and their team members more creative by eliminating workplace fears.

🔑 Key Takeaways

- 🔒 Leadership support should be apparent when senior leaders actively promote innovation programs. Open support improves team members' confidence levels and strengthens wide-spread participation rates.

🔓 The removal of cumbersome approval procedures results in faster innovative performance, which results in better efficiency.

🔓 When leaders establish open lines of honesty, they produce innovative teams that build stronger relationships.

💡 Lessons Learned

🔖 Senior leadership roles significantly influence the development of an organization's culture. Leaders' innovative support leads to increased team participation and greater innovation success.

🔖 A leader's speed influences project momentum and team member enthusiasm by enabling quick decision-making.

🔖 Open and encouraging connections from leaders help build stronger relationships of trust while fostering continuous innovative growth.

Strong leadership sets the tone for innovation. Now, here's how senior leaders can put these lessons into action.

🗣 Practical Advice

At 12 Wing, leaders were key in encouraging innovation. They didn't just support change; they also made it easier by removing obstacles, providing resources, and creating a space for ideas to grow. Their dedication to overcoming challenges and backing new projects made innovation a reality. The results of this leadership approach can be seen in the success stories of the 12 Wing Innovation Program.

CHAPTER 9

IMPACT AND SUCCESS STORIES FROM THE 12 WING INNOVATION PROGRAM

"The only way to discover the limits of the possible is to go beyond them into the impossible."

ARTHUR C. CLARKE

The innovation drive at 12 Wing involved idea creation and the practical implementation of those concepts to reshape our operational procedures and organizational structure values.

The following section showcases achievement stories that illustrate how fundamental yet powerful concepts have created significant changes throughout 12 Wing Shearwater. The case studies demonstrate how innovation fosters resource preservation while enhancing staff morale and operational effectiveness.

Through these real-life stories, you can gain practical tools and motivation to replicate such achievements in your organization. The following text examines how workplace transformations occurred through innovative changes.

How 100 Initial Idea Submissions Sparked Big Changes

Inaugurating the 12 Wing Innovation Program, we were uncertain about the outcomes we might achieve. Our modest goal was to obtain a few projects, regardless of their number, as we considered them successful. The idea submission process yielded remarkable results, as we received over 100 suggestions from all sectors across the Wing within a few months. Each proposed idea, regardless of its initial size, had the potential to drive meaningful organizational change. I will explain step by step what transpired and all the ways these small thoughts led to significant results change.

Small Ideas, Big Impact

At first, many people thought that small changes wouldn't make a big difference. However, it soon became obvious that important changes could come from small rather than huge solutions. Small improvements can lead to major changes that can change an entire organization.

The first hundred proposals offered clear benefits that helped this growth.

Bottomup BREAKTHROUGH

◇ Building Momentum

Quick changes happen quickly because they take less time to implement. This speed helps staff feel more confident in sharing new ideas.

◇ Empowering Members

New members suggested many ideas, even though they initially hesitated to share their thoughts. By including their suggestions, they changed from passive participants to active contributors.

◇ Creating Cultural Change

The organization quickly transformed its culture through small achievements. Employees began to see innovation as a key part of their main tasks, integrating daily improvements into their work routines.

◉ Lessons Learned

> Early, successful, rapid solutions will encourage more personnel to get involved. When individuals experience immediate positive results, they stay committed to their tasks.

Small, small changes can create big results. When organizations celebrate quick wins and show appreciation to their team members, they can encourage ongoing innovation. Let's look at simple ways to invite small ideas and maintain progress.

🗣 Practical Advice

Ensure the idea submission process is as brief and straightforward as possible. A clear submission procedure boosts the chances of people participating. Your organization values every idea, regardless of its impact scale. Acknowledging contributions encourages members to stay engaged through feelings of appreciation.

Foster Success Stories

Sharing success stories inspires others and shows how small ideas can make a big difference. At 12 Wing Shearwater, the first 100 idea submissions showed that even simple suggestions can lead to important changes. When team members see their ideas making a difference, they become more involved in innovation.

One ordinary day at 12 Wing Shearwater, an unexpected moment shifted my perspective entirely—showing just how powerful recognition can be.

Recognizing Contributions: The 1 CAD Commander's Coin Award

An ordinary day at 12 Wing Shearwater turned surprising when my assumptions changed unexpectedly.

An Unexpected Moment

As I took my seat to listen, I noticed an email about a routine briefing on forced modernization. I learned that the presentation would focus on this topic. Regular briefings were common at 12 Wing, so I paid attention. Once I was settled, the main topic was force modernization. I'm particularly interested in opera-tions improvement, so I focused intently on the RCAF's challenges in filling project management roles.

The General's Surprise

General Huddleston raised concerns during a briefing about hiring skilled officers, especially Captains, for key project management roles in Force Modernization. He hoped to fill these positions with qualified technicians, although he doubted they could handle the tasks. I couldn't help but smile because I was a skilled technician with a recent Project Management Professional (PMP) certification.

The General then talked about the achievements of the 12 Wing Innovation team, noting that they had received 75 submissions. I thought Nick would be recognized, which he deserved, as he effectively removed barriers to innovation. The General praised the 75 submissions as a significant achievement.

Then, unexpectedly, he asked me to join him on stage to receive the 1 Canadian Air Commanders Coin. I was surprised but curious to learn that this recognized my innovative contributions at 12 Wing. While accepting the honour, I found it ironic, given his earlier comments about project managers. As he handed me the coin, I leaned in and said, "Oh, by the way, I'm a technician with my PMP certification."

His reaction was delightful; he smiled and nodded, enjoying the moment's humor.

🔑 Key Takeaways

- 🔒 Team members respond positively to recognition, whether through public praise or bonuses, which helps keep them engaged.
- 🔒 Active organizations usually have all the skills their members need, but these talents can go unnoticed unless identified. Ongoing engagement and an understanding of each person's abilities can significantly boost performance.
- 🔒 Opportunities can appear unexpectedly, so always being prepared is important. Everyday situations can reveal individual skills and open new career growth paths.

🛠️ Practical Tip

Checkups should be scheduled regularly to publicly acknowledge team members for their job performance, irrespective of their achievements. Recognition boosts dedication and fosters enthusiasm in the workplace.

Always strive to learn about team members' unique skills and certifications through active inquiry. Look directly at those who collaborate with you to identify the specific competencies you require.

Encourage team members to pursue relevant credentials by providing external encouragement for

their professional development. A financial investment in professional training enables organizations to
address current challenges and anticipate future
obstacles.

💡 Lessons **Learned**

- 📌 Recognizing employees' achievements fosters
  team spirit and promotes ongoing product
  development.
- 📌 You should regularly assess your team members' skills to uncover new abilities that create
  opportunities.
- 📌 Your team holds the key to addressing critical
  challenges, and fostering open communication
  channels with team members fosters the
  discovery of effective solutions.

🗣️ **Practical Advice**

- ☑ Hold regular team events for members to share
  their qualifications and work experience.
  During these events, use simple recognition
  programs to celebrate individual achievements
  with awards and tokens.
- ☑ Conduct team surveys and informal discussions
  so members can showcase their certificates
  and skills.

A routine morning turned into a valuable lesson on the
importance of recognition and our team's hidden
talents. By acknowledging our members while looking

for new talent, we increased motivation and found creative solutions to our biggest challenges. The insights gained today can help you drive growth in your organization, so embrace them now.

Pitching to the RCAF Commander: What It Meant for the Program

As Nick and I ran the 12 Wing Innovation Program, I focused on documenting our progress on RCAF rcafé, a platform for open discussion and collaboration within the Air Force. My dedication to transparency and communication, values shaped by LCol Baldasaro's guidance during Plan Qulliq, helped us build trust in our program. Our regular updates caught the attention of senior leaders, leading to the launch of the Vector Check Challenge, a competition to showcase innovation from selected Wings. Only three Wings were chosen to present, making it a unique chance for high-level recognition within the RCAF.

With a strong foundation in our innovation team, Nick recommended that I represent 12 Wing in the challenge. I accepted this opportunity, understanding it was more than just a competition—it was a chance to validate our efforts and demonstrate the impact of grassroots innovation. Before the RCAF Commander and senior leaders, I shared our achievements, showing how empowering members, removing barriers, and encouraging collaboration had changed our approach to challenges. This moment was the highlight of my military career—not because of personal success, but because it showed that true innovation comes not from **Orders** but from people who are free and supported to solve problems in meaningful ways.

The Pitch: Sharing Our Story

The day of the Vector Check Challenge pitch arrived, and I felt ready, thanks to Nick's planning and leadership. Leading up to the event, he organized a full practice run with every Commanding Officer in 12 Wing so I could improve my delivery and prepare for tough questions. I also did two dry runs with the Plan Qulliq team, whose feedback helped refine my approach. This preparation was crucial, changing my pitch from a simple presentation into a strong argument for bottom-up innovation.

When the time came, we presented our program's key principles, showcasing the tools, processes, and real successes that allowed members of 12 Wing to innovate from the ground up. Although we didn't win the official prize, the real success was spreading our message—showing senior RCAF leaders that the solutions to organizational problems are already within our people. Innovation doesn't need huge outside investments; it just needs to remove obstacles, use available resources, and give individuals the trust and freedom to make real changes.

Impact Beyond Winning

12 Wing did not win first place in the competition, but the response afterward was outstanding. Leaders in

the RCAF and their teams from different Wings showed great interest in our success by asking for help to achieve similar outcomes. This experience proved that bottom-up innovation can succeed in any RCAF area, emphasizing its potential for the wider community.

🔑 Key Takeaways

- 🔒 True triumph goes beyond merely finishing first: As sharing knowledge to inspire others represents a genuine victory.
- 🔒 Openly sharing work progress allows others to gain knowledge, encouraging collaboration and fostering new ideas.
- 🔒 Organizations can achieve substantial outcomes using their current resources without investing more money or hiring additional staff members.

💡 Lessons Learned

- 🔨 The open sharing and global promotion of information foster innovation growth and facilitate organizational collaboration.
- 🔨 Your impact and ability to drive change, among others, define your true success, going beyond formal recognition.
- 🔨 Your organization should make the most of the tools already at its disposal. Improved resource management in current operations is as

effective as substantial new investments in innovation.

🗣 Practical Advice

☑ Start by showcasing tangible achievements to highlight the value of your design proposals. Share clear steps for others to use your innovative ideas effectively. Involve more teams and leaders in your training to foster improvements and promote innovation.

☑ Presenting to the RCAF Commander was a key moment that showcased our team's commitment and spurred innovation throughout the organization. By sharing practical methods, we encouraged others to adopt our strategies. The best results come from inspiring ideas in others, not just from winning competitions.

4 Ways How This Model Can Be Replicated in Other Organizations

The bottom-up innovation framework created by 12 Wing works well in the military and helps various organizations. It focuses on improving team communication, continuous development, and empowering employees. This model relies on current workplace tools and staff, avoiding expensive changes and complex reorganizations.

1. The project management office (PMO) should include innovation strategies.

Organizations with Project Management Offices (PMOs) find it easier to adopt bottom-up innovation. They need to set up simple processes that make it easy for employees to share their ideas.

OMB-Mineral Managed Processes (MVPs) are key versions of solutions that organizations should test before using them widely. Adopting Agile Principles allows faster feedback to enhance processes.

This helps top leaders understand improvements from operational areas, creating a clear channel for innovation.

2. Create an Internal Innovation Team for extra responsibilities.

A lean innovation team can grow naturally without a PMO. Organizations can form a team, select employees interested in problem-solving, and add innovative tasks to their roles.

Employees should have chances to lead improvement projects, which builds leadership skills and strategic thinking. Team members must align with the organization's mission and values during hiring. This approach boosts employee morale and encourages a proactive culture without high costs.

3. New Approaches Attract and Retain Workers

Workplace culture is often overlooked, with organizations focusing too much on salaries and benefits. Bottom-up innovation helps by giving employees more control over solving problems, improving their job satisfaction and sense of owner-ship.

Job satisfaction increases when employees feel their contributions are recognized. Organizations are seen as innovative in attracting and keeping top talent while reducing turnover costs.

4. Innovation as a Self-Funding Strategy

The need for innovation doesn't have to come with high costs. When implemented correctly, innovative methods can save money. Employee-driven solutions focus on reducing waste by improving processes and cutting out unnecessary steps.

Quick problem-solving helps businesses maintain steady production. Introducing innovation becomes easier, and employees are less resistant to changes. This system encourages ongoing innovation, allowing businesses to view their innovations as investments rather than costs.

💡 Lessons Learned

- Simplifying innovation at affordable cost requires proper design procedures and easy-to-use tools.
- Employees who believe they are progressing perform at high levels and remain continuously within the organization.

🗣 Practical Advice

- ☑ Make your idea submission system and innovation processes easy to navigate. Regular discussions about achievements and gathering feedback are key to progress, so show appreciation for all contributions to keep employees engaged.

To successfully implement individual-led innovation, it must be embedded into structures like PMOs or supported through dedicated roles. Unlocking your team's potential can drive lasting, meaningful change. Ultimately, creating a culture that empowers innovation strengthens the organization and enhances the growth and success of its people.

CONCLUSION: INNOVATION STARTS WITH YOU

Innovation isn't just for executives or research labs. It happens when ordinary people challenge the status quo and take action.

Throughout this book, we've explored:

- ✓ How bottom-up innovation drives change
- ✓ Why agency and empowerment fuel creativity
- ✓ How to break communication silos and turn ideas into results
- ✓ Real-world examples of how small ideas create massive impact

But knowing this isn't enough. Now, it's your turn.

Your Challenge: Take One Small Action

Before closing this book, ask yourself:

- *What's one inefficient process you see every day?*

- *What's one small change that could make things better?*
- *Who do you need to talk to make it happen?*

Change doesn't require permission. It starts with one person deciding to act.

Gratitude for Mentors and Support

I am very thankful to LCol Baldasaro, LCol Veenhof, LCol Lawrence, Col Holmes, and CWO Wezenbeek. Their leadership and support show that great leaders don't just manage—they create opportunities for innovation and growth.

To my colleagues at 12 Wing, your teamwork has shown me that innovation is not done alone—it's a group effort.

To my wife Jazmin, my son Mikael, and my daughters Jade and Jillian—your love and support are my biggest strengths. You inspire me to keep moving forward, even during tough times.

💡 Lessons Learned

- ✒ You don't need to be an expert to start—innovation begins with a willingness to learn.
- ✒ Great leaders are also great followers—we constantly shift between leading and learning.
- ✒ Mentorship is a catalyst for growth—the right guidance accelerates your potential.

⚒ Collaboration fuels creativity—two minds working together always outperform one.

🗣 **Practical Advice**

- ☑ Seek mentors who challenge you. The best mentors push you to think bigger while supporting your growth
- ☑ Commit to continuous learning. Innovators aren't born—they develop their skills over time.
- ☑ Trust yourself. Imposter syndrome is natural, but your unique experiences and insights are valuable.

Final Thought

Be that person. Start small. Experiment. Improve. And when you succeed, empower others to do the same.

Innovation isn't a theory—it's a habit. Make it yours. You need to trust in your ability regardless of imposter syndrome because your unique history and approach to life turn into assets rather than problems.

If you require assistance implementing the methods outlined in this book, please do not hesitate to contact me at Rich@Bottom-up.ca.

Innovation isn't a theory—it's a habit. Make it yours!

FINAL TWIST

A PERSONAL REFLECTION

Oh, and if you haven't noticed—I never mentioned my rank throughout this book.

I'm **Master Corporal** Dunbar, and when my journey began, I was a **Corporal.** I didn't hold an official leadership title or possess high-level authority. However, I had an idea, the determination to act on it, and the support of incredible mentors and teammates who helped turn it into reality.

I certainly didn't achieve this on my own. Numerous individuals guided, challenged, and believed in me throughout the process. This book isn't merely about my success—it's about what we can accomplish when we adopt innovation from the grassroots level.

All proceeds from this book will be donated to Landing Strong, a Nova Scotia-based non-profit that provides comprehensive mental health support to veterans and first responders.